Making Money
on Blogging

How to Start Your Blogging Blueprint and
Make Profit Online With Your Blog

2020 edition

How do People make Money Blogging?
How I make Money Blogging?

A step-by-step guide for beginners

Best Financial Freedom Books & Audiobooks

By
Robert Kasey

Table of Contents

Introduction

The world has recorded tremendous growth in the last couple of years – especially within this century and the previous. We have seen widespread technological advancements – we have also seen a lot of paradigm shifts that have happened as a result of the many advances in technology. Technology has undoubtedly affected the way we do most things. It has transformed the way we communicate, eat, travel, etc. One area where technology has changed our mode of operation is in the way we interact with one another.

Before the advent of the internet, a lot of people were used to keeping diaries – such diaries were usually written on notepads or notebooks and held securely to prevent loss or damage. However, with the invention of online storage mediums and the internet, people could now keep digital diaries in the form of blogs on the internet. Such digital journals saved on the internet can be accessed repeatedly.

There is no single area of our lives that technology has not affected. In the past, it was wrong for a proper gentleman to walk up to a lady in a gathering and open a conversation with her. The duo (man and lady) would need to be introduced to each other by a third party. However, today, the reverse has become the case – with apps like Tinder, people can arrange a "meet n greet" or other forms of dates by just tapping some buttons on their mobile device while sitting in the comfort of their bedrooms.

Technology has also changed the way we make money – in the past centuries, to make money, one would have to either get a job or start a business. None of these options was as simple as we just made it seem – to get a job, you would need to get a college degree, which cost a lot of money. After graduating from college, you would need to start competing for the few available jobs. To start a business, on the other hand, you would need a lot of money as well.

However, money-making has become increasingly easier today – thanks to the internet, people, both young and old could now sit in the comfort of their living room, wearing nothing more than briefs, and earn as much money as they desire. Several online earning models are available, which the average person can leverage and create a consistent stream of income for him/herself. One of these online business models is blogging. Yes, you heard that right, BLOGGING.

People often think that blogging is an outdated way of making money on the internet – however, nothing can be farther from the truth than that assertion. Blogging has been a viable way of making money online and will continue to be a significant online money spinner for those who know how to do it right. The problem when it comes to making money with blogging is that people are not willing to treat their blog like a business. Remember, anything you do not handle as a business will not pay you like a business.

To put things in the right perspective, people have always rumored that real estate is no longer a viable business that can make you money. However, there are still millions of people who are making millions every day by directly investing in real estate. There will always be naysayers and those who are willing to do the work – while the former group will be there giving reasons why it is not possible, the latter group will be smiling to the bank every day.

The term "blog" was originally derived from the word, "weblog," which is a combination of web and log. It is essentially a log that is hosted on the web for easier and secure access. The word log means a record of day to day events. Gradually, weblog was shortened to blog. Initially, people used blogs as online diaries, where they update things that mattered to them. You would see people posting about their life, things that happen in their home, their travel experiences on their blogs.

Gradually, blogs shifted from just what people used to keep online diaries to what can be used to write about general issues. Today, we have blogs that talk about politics, business, relationships, religion, etc. After blogs shifted from just being online diaries, a lot has happened – people have found a way of monetizing their blogs. Since the early 2000s, people have been making tons of money from different types of blogs, and that will only continue as humans will keep seeking knowledge, information, and even entertainment till the end of time.

While blog posts used to be centered on the owners, today, you could start a blog and write about business, politics, wildlife, travel or a whole lot of other issues that appeal to you. This means that anyone can start a blog today, grow it, and start making money from it. Starting a blog is no longer exclusively reserved for people who live super exciting lives, like celebrities. Even if your life is not as exciting, there are tons of other things you can share on your blog, monetize the blog and make money.

As mentioned earlier, blogging started as a hobby for some people; however, you can now build a blog and turn it into your own full-time business. We have seen a lot of young and older people do – these people did not do anything spectacular; they only treated their blog as a business, and it started paying them like a business.

If you want to be among those who are currently earning money from blogging, then you are at the right place as this definitive guide is for you. You might think that blogging is saturated but is there really any business in the world that is not saturated? Let's face it; every business you could think of is already saturated and what differentiates those who make it in one business from those who make excuses is the effort they put in.

One good thing with blogging is that if you put in the necessary effort and treat it like a business, it will pay you like a business. On the other hand, if you treat it like a hobby, it will cost you like a hobby. That being said, how do you create a blog and turn it into your personal cash cow? What type of blog do you need to create? What are the various blogging niches available to you? Ultimately, how do you run your blog like an actual business so that it can pay you like a business?

All these and more are what we shall be discussing in this all-encompassing guide. If you have been dreaming of earning money online through blogging, then join this ride. Even if you have been blogging for some time, but you have not recorded success, then it is evident that you are doing something wrong and we shall expose you to the right strategies that if you apply them, you will see your much-desired breakthrough.

Without further ado, let's get started.

Chapter One:

Is blogging really for me?

First of all, anyone that runs a blog is called a blogger – people often have this common misconception that all bloggers are good writers, politically aware, or savvy young chaps who are extremely good at working with computers. This is nothing more than a misconception – the truth is that anybody who can as much as operate a smartphone can venture into blogging and become quite successful at it.

Within the past few years, people from all walks of life, nationality, race, age, etc. have turned bloggers, and that changed their lives for good. One good thing about blogging is that it is vast – there is always something to blog about. If you are not good at analyzing politics, you could be good at writing about dogs, cats, and other pets. If you are not good at explaining sports, you might be good at giving fashion tips. If you are not good at creating and posting food recipes, you might be good at writing travel blog posts. So, this simply means that there is something you can do as a blogger – blogging is not reserved for some select few.

The only thing that could make it hard for you to succeed as a blogger is lack of motivation, determination, perseverance, and focus. It is essential that we mention that while blogging is not a get-rich-quick scheme, if you do it right, however, it has the potential to make you rich, but you must be willing to put in the needed effort.

One mistake that most people who stumble into blogging make is that they think they could create a blog today, monetize it tomorrow and start making money next week. Unfortunately, it does not work that way – your blog is like your typical business, you must give it time, nurture it until it grows into a money-making machine.

Another mistake that people make is that they want to treat their blog as a hobby and expect it to pay them like a business. As mentioned earlier, if you treat what you do like a business, it will pay you like a business, but if you treat it as a hobby, it will pay you as a hobby. While there are people who blog as a hobby, our focus in this book is to raise people who see blogging as a business. Now, if you really want to run a blog as a business, you need a certain level of commitment.

First, you have to see it as if you are running a typical brick and mortar store. Someone that has a brick and mortar store wakes up early in the morning; then they proceed to open their store. After opening the store, they take inventory of available stock; then they open their books for the day. As the day goes by, the store owner discusses with customers, close sales, and at the end of the day, take another inventory, close their book for the day and go home.

Now, if a typical store owner does all that hard work, it means that a blogger has some tasks to do as well. However, the work aspect is what some bloggers do not want to do, but they want to reap the benefits. This is not unconnected to the fact that some acclaimed gurus had sold them some fake dreams in the past. They have been told that you don't need to work to make money online.

So, the answer to the question, "is blogging really for me?" is YES. Blogging can be for you as long you are ready to work. Even if you are not a writer, you could hire writers to do the writing aspect of the blogging business for you. It is also essential to state that writing is just a small fraction of what bloggers do – the more significant part of blogging business involves driving traffic to your blog posts, social media marketing, and attracting brands to advertise their products on your blog so you could earn money. So, even if you are not a writer, you can still do be a blogger – you only need to hire a writer to create the posts for you.

To succeed as a blogger, you need to create a clear roadmap and focus on your goals. With the right motivation, dedication, perseverance, and a learning spirit, you can turn your blog into a money-making machine in a short time.

Chapter Two:
Why start a blog?

There are a million make-money-online schemes that abound out there, so, why should anyone ditch many of those and pitch their tent with blogging? This is a question that any logical person would want to ask. While the other numerous make money online schemes have great potential to make you money, blogging is unique for so many reasons, and we are going to talk about these unique benefits of blogging shortly.

1. Blogging can make you rich

While blogging is not a get rich quick scheme, it does have the potential to make you rich. One good thing about the income you earn from blogging is its passive nature. This means that you only have to do the work once and watch your income keep flowing in even on the days you decide not to work.

With such a passive income model, you can have all the time in the world to bond with your family, take vacations, and do other things that matter to you.

Another thing that makes blogging an excellent money-making business is that there are thousands of ways through which you can make money with your blog. You can sell ad space to advertisers – this is one of the most popular methods of making money with your blog. When it comes to selling ad space – you have many choices. You can let ad networks like Google, Bing, etc. place ads on your blog and pay you on a commission basis or you can develop your own unique pricing model, negotiate with companies directly, have them pay you money to place their advertisements on your blog.

Additionally, you can accept sponsored posts where businesses pay you money to place marketing content on your blog. This is how it works – a company writes a marketing post which they could use to drive traffic to their own website. Then, they pay you money to publish the post on your blog and link it to their website. You can accept as many guest posts as possible in a month, and you earn according to the number of such posts you publish on your blog. Also, how much you can earn through this income model solely lies in your hands. So, the better your negotiation skills, the more money you earn.

You can also promote affiliate offers on your blog and earn a commission when a sale happens through the link you promoted. Affiliate marketing is a highly profitable way of making money on the internet. With affiliate marketing, you do not need to develop a product – you promote the products already developed by other companies to your blog visitors. If a sale happens through your promotions, then the company that has the product pays you an affiliate commission.

Affiliate marketing is always a win-win for both you, the company that owns the product you are promoting and the customer. It is a win for you because you get to earn for promoting other people's products. It is a win for the company that developed the affiliate product because other people help them to promote their goods and services. And it is a win for the customer because you are helping them have access to products that can help them solve their problems.

There are thousands of affiliate marketing networks you can partner with and earn money when you promote their products on your blog. Clickbank.com is a popular affiliate marketing network where you can find millions of products that you can promote to your audience and earn money. You can also consider joining the Amazon affiliate program where you promote Amazon products on your blog so that when people buy those products or even other products through your efforts, Amazon pays you money.

Most of the internet service providers you will be using their service as a blogger have affiliate programs which you can join and earn money by promoting some tools to your audience. For instance, you need a hosting service to host your blog; you also need a domain name provider – the chances are that these providers will have affiliate programs. Now, when you promote their affiliate offers, and people get to buy hosting service through your affiliate links, you earn money.

There are also hundreds of other tools you need as a blogger and most of them have affiliate programs as well. For instance, you need an autoresponder for email marketing purposes, and most autoresponders have affiliate offers you can promote. Apart from the tools you make use of, you can promote a ton of affiliate software tools or products that you think your audience needs.

Another great way through which you can earn money with your blog is by selling digital and physical products. In fact, digital products are best because you don't need to keep inventory – you simply develop a single copy of the product and sell to millions of customers. The difference between a physical and digital product is that you can touch a physical product while you cannot do the same for a digital product. Digital products are held intangibly on offline and online storage mediums. Typical examples of digital products include eBooks, software programs, and digital games. Examples of physical products include wristwatches, shirts, hoverboards, etc.

Now, you don't need to be the developer of either the physical or digital products before you can sell them on your blog. If you want to start selling eBooks on your blog, for instance, you could hire a writer, provide them with an outline and have them create a good eBook which you can host and sell on your blog. As for physical products, you can enter into a partnership with major brands so you can drop ship their products on your blog. Once you have grown your blog's audience, selling products to them will not be a problem, and the return can be quite impressive.

Your blog can make you money through gated content – how this works is – you create some special high quality and high in demand content on your blog, then make it available on a subscription basis to only those readers who pay. You can create a members-only section and hide away the more valuable content there – then when a member pays a stipulated subscription fee, you give them access to the gated member's only section.

While the above is not so popular, there are still some bloggers who earn money through it. However, before you try incorporating such a model into your blog, you need to have grown the blog to a certain level. Obviously, you cannot adopt this model when you are just starting out, and you must have shown that you know your onions as well. If you want to make the model work for you, your free content must be compelling enough and packed with value to make the reader want to pay for more. If your general content is not good enough, no reader would want to pay you money to read more of your content.

The methods described above are some of the most popular means of earning through your blog. There are obviously more ways through which you can make money with your blog; we have just discussed the popular ones. Depending on your audience, you can research and creatively come up with more ways of monetizing your content. In a subsequent section of this book, we shall do an in-depth analysis of each of these blog income models. For now, let's continue to look at the other benefits of running a blog.

2. Blogging will help you improve your writing and technical skills

Blogging gives you a chance to learn and perfect some critical skills, such as writing and other technical skills. Even if you aren't writing your blog posts yourself, you will still be working with some technical tools, and the more you work with these tools, the more you learn and improve. If you are the one writing your posts, blogging will definitely help you to improve your writing skills.

As a blogger, you will be using a lot of plugins and templates – you may also need to learn basic web design so you can always modify your blog without seeking the help of a professional that might be costly. The more you work with these online tools, the more you develop your technical skills.

Additionally, as a blogger, you will always need to do a lot of search engine optimization, email marketing, and content marketing. Learning and perfecting all these skills will not only help you to become a successful blogger, but you can also apply the skills in running your other online businesses.

3. Blogging will help you develop healthier habits

In addition to helping you develop some valuable technical skills, blogging also helps you to learn the art of commitment and discipline. Healthy habits like time management, dedication, etc. which you can learn while blogging can come in handy when you are dealing with other aspects of your personal and professional life. So, blogging does not just put money in your pocket alone; it helps you to develop some critical skills and learn healthy habits.

4. Blogging helps you build a network

When people face a challenge, the first thing they do is that they turn to the internet to seek a solution. By owning a blog and posting useful content, you can attract people who will see you as their hero – these people will consume your content, post their own thoughts in the form of comments, and some will even send you personal messages.

Some of your readers can go all out to arrange a physical meeting with you – all this will increase your network beyond your imagination. Aside from your readers, some brands can get in touch with you through the useful content you create and propose a deal to you. In all, running a blog will help you grow a network of friends and acquaintances that will be helpful to you in the long run.

5. Blogging enables you to increase your knowledge of things in your niche and beyond

There is a hidden researcher in you, and blogging helps to bring him out. As a blogger, you have to research, collate, sort information, and present it authoritatively to your audience. Remember, your readers are visiting your blog because they see you as an authority in your niche. So, you must do the proper research to ensure that you post only quality content. In your bid to put up new well-researched content regularly, your effort will lead you to the discovery of new things in your field and beyond.

6. Blogging gives you the perfect outlet to express yourself

Your blog, no matter the type of content you share with it is still your personal space – so, even if your blog is a niche one, you can still intersperse your opinions in your posts and get your voice heard. You can use your blog to air your opinions on trending issues while still maintaining a defined niche. A blog is a perfect outlet for self-expression.

7. Blogging exposes you to new opportunities and ideas

As a blogger, you will literally live on the internet – this means you will always get exposed to numerous opportunities and ideas that abound on the internet. It could be ideas on ways of making money or improved ways of living a healthier life – blogging just makes you more exposed than the average Joe on the streets. The more you get exposed, your approach to life will change for the better. The people you will get to meet will also influence your life positively, and the fact that you have people who see you as a hero will make you want to be of good behavior.

8. You can make a difference in people's lives

Millions of people around the world are facing one issue or the other, and they usually turn to the internet to seek a solution. These people are just looking for a little glimmer of hope or something to give them assistance in the midst of their despair and gloom. Even without your knowing it, your blog could be the tonic that someone needs to get their life back.

The above are just some of the few benefits of blogging – in the next sections of this guide, we shall talk about different blogging niches and how to choose the one that is best for you.

Chapter Three:
Getting started

If you have decided that blogging is something you would want to do, then welcome to this chapter where we shall introduce you to the first things you need to do as a blogger.

If you want to go to college, for instance, there are some things you must do first before the others. For example, you need to first decide on the course you want to study, check with the admissions office, fill some forms, write a statement of purpose, etc. After you have been offered admission, you proceed to accept the offer, do the necessary registrations, pay the required fees, and then start your studies.

The same way no one just wakes up one day and starts attending college, that's the same way you should not just wake up one morning and start blogging. Blogging is a serious business, at least for now, and it requires a lot of planning on your part. You need to plan on what to blog about, how to attract traffic to your blog posts, how to monetize your blog, and how to scale up your blogging business.

First things first – choose a niche

When people go to college, they study only one course out of the millions available in the school. The reason is simple – you cannot conveniently study all the courses that the University offers, you must choose one, stick with it, and excel at it. Even as you continue with your studies, you are further mandated to specialize in a specific area of interest in your field.

Now, the same way you cannot study all the courses in the university, it is not advisable for you to create a blog and write about all the random topics that come to your mind. No, there has to be order – people should know your blog for something such that when they need that particular thing, your blog becomes their go-to place.

If you have an ear infection, for instance, and you visit the hospital to get help, which of the following doctors would you rather allow to attend to you?

Doctor A: a general practitioner who diagnoses and treats all kinds of common ailments.

Doctor B: an ear, nose, and throat (ENT) specialist who is an expert at treating ear, nose, and throat infections.

Typically, you would go for doctor B because he is a specialist and is more likely to understand what is wrong with you.

If you really want to make money blogging, then you must find a niche and stick with it. Finding a blog niche might sound easy, but it is not as easy. It is the important first step you need to take before everything else. Although you can always switch to another niche later in the future, it is better to get it right once.

Your blog niche will be determined by the type of audience you want to serve. Once you know your audience, it will be easier for you to create blog posts and other types of products that satisfy their needs. Importantly, having a defined niche will help you to maintain focus, so you don't write on sports today and write on entertainment tomorrow. It will also help you determine the best marketing strategies for you – this is because the type of blog you have will significantly impact the blog income opportunities available to you. That being said, what is a niche?

What is a niche?

A niche has to do with interests, services, or products that only appeal to a small, specialized segment or section of a larger audience or population. It can also be said to be the smaller part of a larger whole.

In the above definition, you will notice some keywords which include "specialized," and "larger audience" or "population." When you look at the everyday uses of those keywords, it will be easier for you to understand what a niche really means. For instance, the word "sport" is extensive and consists of different types of sporting events.

Now, when you talk about sports, you will begin to see that there are different types which include soccer, basketball, baseball, etc. These different types of sports are niches within the broad category. Even within the niches, you can still narrow down each niche – for instance, within baseball, you can find "major league baseball," and "national baseball." All these are sub-niches within the baseball niche.

When it comes to blogging, your niche is the overarching topic that you focus your blog contents on. It is more like the umbrella category that houses and defines the types of content you will be publishing on your blog. For instance, soccer is quite a broad niche; you can narrow down and blog about European football leagues. You can narrow down further and blog about European league predictions.

Why does your blog need a niche?

This is an important question we must answer before proceeding. Why does your blog need a niche? Why can't you just blog on something as broad as soccer, for instance? Why can't you just blog on how to make money online? Why can't you just blog on how to prepare delicious meals?

Your blog needs to focus on a specific niche for several reasons, and these reasons are not hard to guess – we have already named some of them earlier. Picture yourself in a large hall filled with people saying different things – everybody in the hall wants to be heard. Now, picture yourself in another small room where there are only five people – everybody in this small room wants to be heard too. Which of these places do you think that your voice stands a higher chance of being heard?

Obviously, in the large hall, everybody will be shouting, trying to get their voice heard, and this will make it extremely hard for your own voice to make an impact because it will get buried in the midst of other voices. However, in the small room, since there are only about five people, you stand a higher chance of getting your voice heard. This is just the perfect explanation of why you need a niche for your blog.

If your blog is targeting a broad audience, it will be tough for you to draw traffic to it. It will also be hard for you to make money through affiliate sales – this is not to mention that your search engine ranking will suffer. Such broad niches have already been monopolized by early starters in the game or the big fishes in the ocean of blogging. As a starter, you will find it extremely hard to compete with all the established blogs that are already targeting those broad niches.

Targeting a general niche is also bad for engagement. When you blog about a broad topic, you will most likely attract people who are not quite interested in what you are saying, and this will affect user engagement on your blog negatively. So, from the very beginning, you need to define your niche and stick with it. For instance, instead of blogging on ways of making money online, narrow down and blog on one of the options or suggestions being made. There are many ways of making money online, and if you focus on one, your blog will record higher traffic and engagement.

With a niche blog, you will have a defined audience; you will understand what they truly need and feed them accordingly. For instance, if you create a blog that focuses on back pain, people who have back pain will easily relate to what you are saying and follow all your posts. Since you already know the kind of people you are dealing with, you won't waste time creating other types of posts that won't appeal to them.

Also, if you are blogging about a small audience, it is easy for you to truly understand all the problems they are facing so you can speak to them directly. When your readers notice that you are talking about the specific issues they are facing, it will be easier for them to trust you as an authority in the field.

With that said, let's look at some of the ways of finding a perfect niche for your blog.

How to find a blog niche

When it comes to finding a blog niche, you have two options – to go with the most popular niches that everyone talks about or to find your own niche that appeals to you. Some of the most popular blog niches arranged in no particular order include:

- Technology

- DIY/Home Décor

- Beauty & Fashion

- Finance

- Self-Help

- Dating & Relationships

- Making Money Online

- Weight Loss

- Fitness

- Health

One problem with all the popular niches above is that they are quite broad and their competitive score is high as well. When most people want to start a blog, the typical blog about these mentioned competitive niches, and that's the reason why they are very saturated. If you start blogging about any of the niches, you would hardly record success. Your blog will find it challenging to rank on search engines – hence, you will have to spend a lot of money on pay per click advertising.

Instead of blogging in any of the competitive niches, you can take one of the niches, break it down further and continue to narrow your search until you get to a sub-niche within the niche that is yet to be saturated. For instance, "car" is a broad name – and under it, you will get Mercedes Benz, Volkswagen, BMW, etc. If you take Mercedes Benz, for instance, which is a type of car, you will find out that even within that sub-niche, you will find Mercedes Benz S-Class Coupe, GLE Coupe, etc. When you focus on GLE Coupe, for instance, you may still differentiate them by the model year. This is a perfect example of how to breakdown a broad niche until it becomes very narrow and less competitive.

When it comes to choosing a blog niche, you have to take any of the competitive niches, then break it down until you get a very narrow sub-niche. In online business terms, this is called niching down – because it is like climbing from the bottom of a tree and finding one of the numerous branches on the tree to sit on.

Here are the steps you need to take to find the perfect blog niche:

Step 1: Consider your interests

This sounds clichéd, but for you to succeed in something like blogging, you cannot underestimate the importance of blogging in a niche that interests you. Remember, you will be positioning yourself as an authority – and if what you are blogging about is of interest to you, you will often go the extra mile to research and give you readers valuable content.

In life, we all have various interests – some of us are interested in music, sports, business, etc. If you know how to make money online or how to fish, you can turn that into your blog niche. Look inwards; there must be that one thing that you can talk about very well, even without consulting a source — the next thing you need to do is to convert this your interest into your blog niche.

Next, open a text editor on your computer or open a new page on your notepad, then write down the phrase, "blog niche ideas." Move to the next two lines and list your passions or topics you are interested in blogging about. These topics could include your general interests, hobbies, passions, etc. Make sure you list as many as you want.

Now, under each interest, start listing more child branches by thinking of specific topics or subtopics based on what you know best. This is one of the reasons you are advised to go for a niche that is of interest to you instead of one that you perceive is profitable. If you choose a niche that is of importance to you, you will be able to produce a lot of useful content, and this will increase your chances of succeeding as a new blogger.

Additionally, when you are blogging in a niche that interests you, posting content will not be a problem. You will easily create new content that your visitors will love to read – even though you don't post every day, your readers will always be confident that anytime you post, the content will be top quality.

Furthermore, your readers want you to solve their problem, and how are you going to do that if you don't understand the kind of issues they have or if their problem doesn't interest you? If you blog about your passion and what you know, you will easily connect with your readers and speak personally to them.

So, once you have listed a passion, interest, or blog idea, and you have also listed many branches under each of the topics, proceed to add more child branches to the existing ones. You don't need to be a perfect expert on any of the child branches – you only need to have some fair knowledge on them, at least. For instance, if one of the broad topics you have chosen is "baseball" and you only know some rules of the game, then that's okay as there are people who don't even know these rules and they can find your blog useful.

Example.

Let's assume that your broad topic is fishing; under that, you can get ice fishing and fly fishing. Now, both fly fishing and ice fishing are both branches of the main niche. For each of these branches, continue to narrow your search and find more child branches. For instance, if you focus on ice fishing, you could have trout fishing, walleye fishing, and bass fishing. Under fly fishing, you could have bass fishing and trout fishing as well. You might consider taking each of the child branches and niche down the more until you have arrived at a narrower topic.

In the above example, the broad topic "fishing" was narrowed down until we got child branches like "trout fishing." If you want to consider any of the branches or child branches, you need to examine it and see if you could turn it into a whole blog. For instance, if you have chosen "bass fishing," can you possibly create a year's worth of content around that topic or niche? That's a critical question you should ask yourself before settling for any sub-niche.

Step 2: Use a keyword planner to get more ideas

If you are finding it hard to break down your chosen niche or topic into sub-topics or child branches, then you can use Google Keyword Planner to get ideas. Google Keyword Planner is owned by Google and incorporated into its advertisement platform. To use the tool, you will need to log in with your Google account or Gmail details. If you don't have a Google account, you can create one by visiting mail.google.com.

When you type some broad keywords into the Keyword Planner, the tool will return a list of possible child branches of the topic. This way, you can get a clear idea of sub-niches available within the niche.

To use the Keyword Planner, you simply need to visit ads.google.com, use your google account to log in. On the homepage that greets you upon login, click on "Tools," then "Keyword Planner." To conduct new keyword research, click on "Find new keywords," then enter a seed niche idea you want to get information about. See image below.

The results you will get from the keyword research will look like the image below. "Ice fishing" was used as the seed keyword for this example.

	Keyword (by relevance)	Vol (US)	CPC (US)	Comp (US)	Avg. monthly searches	Competition
☐	ice fishing ☆ 🗑	22,200	$0.58	0.27	10K – 100K	Low
☐	ice fishing gear ☆ 🗑	12,100	$0.75	1	10K – 100K	High
☐	ice shanty ☆ 🗑	18,100	$0.54	0.58	10K – 100K	Medium
☐	ice fishing house 🗑	3,600	$0.68	1	1K – 10K	High
☐	ice fishing shanty 🗑	4,400	$0.40	1	1K – 10K	High
☐	ice fishing shelter 🗑	2,900	$0.49	1	1K – 10K	High
☐	ice fishing equipme… 🗑	1,000	$0.71	1	1K – 10K	High
☐	ice fishing clothing 🗑	1,000	$0.76	1	1K – 10K	High
☐	ice fishing jigs ☆ 🗑	2,400	$0.23	1	1K – 10K	High
☐	ice fishing tent ☆ 🗑	3,600	$0.38	1	1K – 10K	High
☐	ice fishing tackle ☆ 🗑	720	$0.37	1	100 – 1K	High

You can take any of the sub-niches shown in the image and turn it into your blog niche. Again, you will need to be sure that the topic can be developed into a whole blog. This you can do by ensuring that you can create a year's worth of blog posts around the subject.

You can enter each niche idea you have into the tool and generate as many sub-niches as possible. Once you are done, proceed to select one or two ideas from the numerous ones you have gotten.

Step 3: Determine which niche is most profitable

You may decide to choose a niche from the research and brainstorming you have done so far. However, you can still do further research to find the profitability of any niche you want to choose before settling for it.

One tool that helps you to research the profitability of a niche, topic, or keyword is Keyword Everywhere. It is a browser extension that you install on your Chrome or Firefox browser. What the extension does is that anytime you do a Google search, it will show you the number of people searching for that keyword or term in a month. The tool will also show you how much advertisers are willing to pay for the keyword or phrase.

For instance, let's search for "walleye fishing" on Google using a browser that has the Keyword

Everywhere extension installed. See screenshot below for the result of the search.

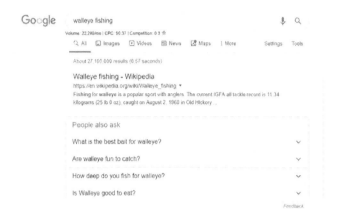

In the screenshot, you can see that 22,200 people search for Walleye fishing in a month, and CPC, which is the amount that advertisers are willing to pay for the keyword is $0.37. The keyword also has a competitive score of 0.3.

Now, what you need to do is – install Keyword Everywhere extension on your browser and type all your selected blog niche ideas into Google. Click on the search button and record the figures returned by the extension in a spreadsheet or Word document.

See screenshot below.

Walleye Fishing
- **Search Volume:** 18,100 searches/month
- **CPC:** $0.39

Trout Fishing
- **Search Volume:** 14,800 searches/month
- **CPC:** $1.66

Bass Fishing
- **Search Volume:** 49,500 searches/month
- **CPC:** $0.52

Ice Fishing
- **Search Volume:** 22,200 searches/month
- **CPC:** $0.58

Fly Fishing
- **Search Volume:** 90,500 searches/month
- **CPC:** $1.38

In the above document, we recorded the search volume and CPC for each niche idea we are using for this example.

Next, after you have determined the number of people searching for each blog niche idea and the CPC of the keyword, you need to review the popularity of the niche idea over time. If a topic has just gained popularity over the past few months, then you don't want to create a blog about that topic because it will soon fade away the same way it gained popularity suddenly. You also don't want to create a blog about a topic that is already dying. Your best bet is to choose a niche that has maintained its popularity consistently for many years.

The best tool for testing the popularity of blog niche topic or idea is Google Trends – it is a tool by Google. To use the tool, visit trends.google.com, enter a keyword of interest, and you will see how the keyword has fared in terms of popularity over the months.

The screenshot below shows the popularity of "walleye fishing."

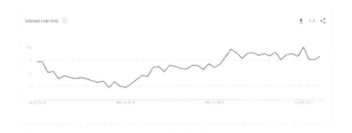

In the above screenshot, you can see that the popularity of the keyword dropped around November 2018. Ideally, you wouldn't want to choose a niche that doesn't attract consistent traffic throughout the year. Instead, you should continue your research and find other keywords or niche topics that are relatively popular throughout the seasons of a typical year.

So, enter the other topic ideas you have into Google Trends and observe how they maintained popularity throughout the year. Since we are using different types of fishing for this example, we may need to search for "ice fishing." Typically, ice fishing will be more popular around the winter months, so you may need to search for other topic ideas. You need to keep searching until you find a niche topic or idea that trends all through the year or for most of the year.

After you have sieved out some topic ideas, you should be left with just a handful. You still need to test the remaining ones for popularity on social media, and you can do that using Buzzsumo. Buzzsumo is a tool that shows you the amount of engagement (likes, shares, etc.) that a particular topic or keyword records on different social media platforms.

To check a keyword on Buzzsumo, visit the website, then in the search bar, type the keyword or niche topic, and hit "Go." The site will list current conversations on social media that contain the topic or keyword you just entered. Additionally,, the tool will show you how many likes, shares, comments the keyword has received on each social media platform. The result the website will return will look like the screenshot below.

Now, go back to your spreadsheet where you recorded each niche topic as well as the information you have gathered about them. Next, include the popularity (on Google Trends and Buzzsumo) of each of the niche ideas.

Check the sale potential of the niche idea

At this point, you should be getting close to having one particular niche topic or idea that is most viable among the various options you have. The next thing you need to do is to check the niche topic's sale potential on platforms like Amazon and Udemy. The reason for checking on Amazon is that eBooks are among the most popular products developed by bloggers. So, if there are already eBooks in your preferred niche that are selling well on Amazon, it means that the niche topic has a high sales potential.

So, head on to Amazon, go to the eBook category; in the search box; type your preferred niche topic or idea. Sort your search by indicating that the books with the most reviews should appear first. Note the number of reviews that the first two books that show up in the results have. Repeat this process for all your niche ideas – then sieve out the niche ideas that have books with a few reviews.

Check for competition

The last thing you need to check before settling for a particular niche is the page authority and domain authority of the blogs that are already existing in the niche. A free method to do that involves creating a free account on moz.com and installing the MozBar browser extension. The MozBar extension works like Keyword Everywhere.

Search for each of your niche topic on Google; the MozBar extension will return the page authority and domain authority of each of the sites that show up in your Google search results. We are not interested in the page authority; we only want to consider the domain authority of each of the websites that show up in the search results. If the domain authority of a website is high, you will find it hard to compete with such a site.

For each niche topic that you search on Google, record the domain authority of the first website or blog that shows up in the search result. You need to round up the figures to the nearest whole number. If the first search result for any niche idea is a YouTube video, then skip that for the next result or website.

By this time, the spreadsheet you are using to record your figures or results should look like the screenshot below:

Walleye Fishing
- **Search Volume:** 18,100 searches/month
- **CPC:** $0.39
- **Interest Over Time:** popularity decreases in the fall and early winter
- **Most Shares:** 6,300
- **Amazon Reviews:** 34
- **Udemy:** no courses
- **Average DA:** 62

Trout Fishing
- **Search Volume:** 14,800 searches/month
- **CPC:** $1.66
- **Interest Over Time:** popularity decreases in the fall and winter
- **Most Shares:** 26,800 (Youtube); 3,200
- **Amazon Reviews:** 146
- **Udemy:** 1 course; 3 reviews
- **Average DA:** 56

Bass Fishing
- **Search Volume:** 49,500 searches/month
- **CPC:** $0.52
- **Interest Over Time:** popularity decreases in the fall and winter
- **Most Shares:** 10,000
- **Amazon Reviews:** 126
- **Udemy:** no courses
- **Average DA:** 69

Looking at the above screenshot, you will find out that "Fly fishing" and "bass fishing" have the highest search volume. However, the domain authority for the websites that are already available in the different niches is quite high. If you create a blog in such niches, you will find it hard to outcompete the already available blogs or websites.

"Trout fishing" as shown in the screenshot has low search volume, but the average domain authority of the sites already available in the niche is 56, which is okay. Also, the CPC for the niche topic is even higher than that of "Bass fishing" and "Walleye fishing." So, if you want to choose one niche from the three shown in the screenshot above, you are better off settling with "trout fishing" as your blog will have higher chances of ranking on Google if your blog about that niche.

Notice how we have dedicated a lot of time and attention to talk about niches and how to choose one? The reason is simple – once you have gotten this aspect of blogging right, then you can rest assured that you are already halfway into becoming a successful blogger. If, on the other hand, you fail to get this stage right, then it means that your blog had already started failing before it even started.

Now that you have chosen your blog niche, the next thing you need to do is to choose the best blogging platform.

Chapter Four:
Choosing a blogging platform

Once you have chosen your preferred niche, the next step is to choose your preferred blogging platform. The two most popular blogging platforms are WordPress and Blogger (owned by Google). A blogging platform is simply a software that allows you to create, edit, update, delete, or generally manage your blog and posts.

Which of the blogging platforms is better? This is a question that people ask all the time. At the moment, bloggers, web designers seem to have reached a consensus that WordPress is better than Blogger for so many reasons. This is not saying that Blogger is not equally good.

As mentioned earlier, Blogger is owned by Google, and it is an excellent platform for people who want to host a simple blog that they can update and edit easily. Once you have a Gmail account or Google account, then you can create a Blogger account – it is one of Google's integrated services. One good thing about using the Blogger platform is that you don't need to spend money on website hosting anymore. The created blog is automatically hosted by Google, for free.

Furthermore, if you don't want to pay for a custom domain (which is highly not recommended), then you can use a free subdomain provided by Google. Let's assume that the name of your blog is Car Racing; if there is no other blog bearing the same on the Blogger platform, then could choose carracing.blogspot.com as your domain name. The extension ".blogspot.com" is automatically attached to your blog name selected by Google.

If you want to remove the ".blogspot.com" attachment from your URL, you will need to buy a domain name, then redirect your blog on the Blogger platform to your new domain name. If you do that successfully, your new domain name will become "carracing.com." Note: the blog will still be hosted on Google. So, you are only paying for a domain name.

Once you have sorted out your domain name or blog name, you can choose any of Blogger blog themes, customize it as you please and then proceed to upload your first blog post. A theme shows how the different sections of your blog will look when viewed on desktop and mobile. If you don't like any of the default Blogger themes, you can pay for a premium Blogger theme or download one of the many available free Blogger themes on the internet.

One thing that makes many bloggers shy away from Blogger is that it has only limited themes and plug-ins. A lot of bloggers don't use the platform – as a result, theme developers don't find it necessary to develop as many themes for the platform.

Plug-ins allow you to add several interesting features to the existing features of a software. Most software plug-ins are usually developed by a third party to improve the performance or add more functionalities to existing software. There are some plug-ins that when you install them on your WordPress blog will help you share your posts to your different social media pages. Some plug-ins help you maintain the security of your blog. Some plug-ins help you improve the search engine ranking of your blog.

When it comes to plug-ins, Blogger has a minimal number of plug-ins. The reason for that is – since most people are not using the Blogger platform, software developers who develop plug-ins concentrate their efforts on developing plug-ins for WordPress rather than Blogger.

With just a few available and boring themes, many bloggers ditch the Blogger platform for WordPress. Apart from the availability of a wide range of plug-ins and themes to choose from, there are several other reasons that make people prefer WordPress to Blogger. Let's take an in-depth look at WordPress and some of the features that make it great.

WordPress

WordPress is a content management system built using PHP (a programming language) and MySQL (a database management system). One thing that makes WordPress great is that you can install plug-ins for added functionalities. Also, you can make use of thousands of available templates or themes – all this makes it very simple to create or set up a blog using WordPress.

The simplicity of use of WordPress is such that anybody who can send a text message on their mobile phone can use it. All you need is to download and install the content management system on your website host. Proceed to download and install any of the available WordPress themes –

download and install some essential plug-ins – customize the theme according to your taste and start uploading your blog posts.

Many bloggers and website designers also prefer WordPress because of its improved security architecture. If you need added security, you can download and install plug-ins that will help you secure your site from hackers and cyber-attacks.

Also, there are available plug-ins that can help you improve the search engine ranking of your blog. This is another important reason why so many bloggers prefer WordPress. As a blogger, search engine optimization is vital to you because if you write the best blog posts in the world and people do not get to discover and read them, then you have just wasted your efforts. SEO plug-ins that can be installed on WordPress help increase the search engine ranking of your website such that when people are searching for content related to the one you have on your blog; your posts will show up in their search results.

With WordPress, you will always get support whenever you need it. For instance, if you are doing anything on your site and run into a problem or technical difficulty, you could easily search online and find your answers on any of the many available WordPress forums littering the cyberspace. You may also get direct support from the WordPress support team.

Now that you have made up your mind to go with WordPress – next, you need to purchase a domain name and hosting plan.

Domain name

Your domain name is like the physical address of your blog on the internet – it is what visitors will use to locate your blog on the web. An example of a domain name is www.yourblogname.com.

Many people think choosing a domain is such an easy task; however, you will find out when you want to embark on the adventure that it is not as easy as it seems. You may discover that all the names you have been considering have all been taken.

Remember, your domain name is as important as the posts you put up on your blog – it is one of the first things that a visitor notices when they visit your blog. It also helps to improve the search engine ranking of your blog. Additionally, it helps visitors have a clear view of what your blog is all about. If you choose a domain name that does not obviously convey the message of your blog, you may be chasing away visitors.

Here are some tips on finding a good domain name:

Use your niche topic

Since you are starting a niche blog, there is no better domain name than one that contains the keywords in your niche. For instance, if you are blogging about guitars, make sure that "guitars" appear somewhere in your domain name. This way, if visitors come across your domain name, they do not have to think twice before knowing that the blog is about guitars and related stuff.

Unless it is highly necessary, try as much as possible to stay away from hyphenated domain names. Putting a hyphen in your domain name will reduce its smoothness and can be a significant turn off for visitors. Additionally, make sure the name is not unnecessarily prolonged. Once it starts exceeding two words, then it is already getting long. A domain name that consists of three words is already long, and if you try to go more than that, then what you have is a full sentence.

You must also avoid using your name as your domain name unless you are a lifestyle blogger. Even if you are a lifestyle blogger, it might still be necessary for you to separate your name from your business. In the past, some successful bloggers –

both lifestyle bloggers and those in other niches who used their names as their domain names have come out to regret the action.

Neil Patel, a popular blogger and internet marketer, once mentioned that if he were to start all over, he wouldn't use his name as his domain name. So, think twice before using your name as your domain name even if you are a lifestyle blogger.

A ".com" domain is better

The average blog reader already assumes that every website on the internet has a ".com" domain extension. So, when they want to type the URL of a website, they include .com at the end. If your blog uses a different extension, you may be losing visitors, because if your potential visitor attaches the wrong domain extension to your domain name, they will be redirected to a different website and in some cases, the domain name they typed may not even open.

Usually, when bloggers are searching for a domain name, they find out that all the names they have been nursing have all been taken. So, they often decide to choose a different extension as a way of preserving the name they love. It is better for you to still try some other variations of your domain name with the .com extension instead of going for a different extension. While some blogs are doing well with a .net extension, for instance, a .com extension is still your best bet.

Popular websites where you can buy a domain name include Namecheap.com, godaddy.com, namesilo.com, etc.

After choosing a domain name, the next step is to buy a hosting package, install WordPress, download a theme, install some required plug-ins, and start customizing your blog.

Buy a hosting package

We mentioned earlier that your domain name is like the P.O. Box of your blog. Now, your web host is like the container housing the contents of your blog. To understand the difference between your web host and your domain name, let's use a simple illustration.

Let's assume that your blog is your car parked in your garage. If someone wants to find your vehicle, the person must come to your physical address (your domain name), and inside your garage (web host), they will find your car (blog).

Different companies offering web hosting services charge you different amounts to host your blog on their server. One of the best web hosting service providers is Siteground. They have a dedicated hosting service for WordPress websites. You can buy a package for as low as $3.95 per month depending on your unique needs – the number of visitors you expect in a month and the amount of storage space you need. When you are just starting, you may go for a cheaper hosting service and change plans as your blog begins to grow and your traffic improves.

After securing your hosting account, then it is time to install WordPress and get into the proper business of blogging.

Since this book is not about WordPress development, we shall not dedicate a lot of time dwelling on how to setup WordPress blogs. You can find several guides on that topic – we want to concentrate on how to blog for profit. The support section of your web host's website will contain instructions on how you can install WordPress.

After installing WordPress; next, you need to download and install a theme that appeals to you. You can find amazing premium WordPress themes on ThemeForest. While there are free themes that can still work almost like the premium ones, the fact remains that the premium themes are better for several reasons.

They give your blog a more professional look and give you more design options. Remember, your blog is like your business – if you want it to pay you like a business, you have to spend money on it the same way you would spend on your business. After you have installed your preferred theme, then it is time to configure your blog.

As mentioned earlier, this is not a book on WordPress development, so, we shall not be dwelling much on WordPress installation and configuration. However, when designing your blog, there are a few tips you need to follow to improve its professional look, and we have presented some of these tips below.

Font style and size

You need to choose a color and size that will always adapt to the ever-changing resolution of internet-enabled devices. Tacky and cheesy fonts can be a huge turn off for your visitors.

Easy Google Fonts is a WordPress plugin that allows you to modify font style and size in different sections of your blog – consider installing the plugin on your WordPress blog. The plugin also gives you access to hundreds of different font styles.

Color scheme

From the get-go, make sure you decide on the color scheme you want for your blog, and you must stick with this color scheme all through. For instance, if you have chosen blue, white, and black as your preferred color, then you must make sure that you do not use other colors in any section of your blog.

Remember, your blog's color scheme is part of your branding – it is what differentiates your blog from the thousands of others out there. So, it has to be unique, and it also needs to be part of the colors used in your logo.

When choosing a color scheme, make sure it is one that appeals to the visual senses of your audience.

Science has shown that color has some physiological and psychological impacts on a person. Some colors can affect a person's nervous system and cause a change in their emotional state as a result of various hormonal releases. Marketers and business developer have for long been harnessing the potentials inherent in colors to influence the perception of the buy and excite emotions in people.

Your blog niche will go a long way in helping to determine the best color scheme for your blog. Black colors mostly go well with any niche or theme, while blue colors are mostly used for blogs that are more tilted towards career advice and related topics.

White color depicts purity, simplicity, and clarity of purpose, while green simply portrays nature. Pink color shows sensuality, femininity, and love – it is an excellent choice for blogs that talk about relationships and issues of the heart.

Any color you want to adopt for your blog should capture your personality, ideology, and ultimately, your blog niche. A good way to find the best color scheme for your blog is to search for other blogs in the same niche and see the kinds of colors they are using. Do not copy verbatim as you would want to maintain originality still. When you look at the color schemes that others are using, modify them a bit, and come up with your own unique scheme.

Logo

Your blog is your business, and just like any other business, you need to develop a logo which will serve as your branding tool and a means of identification. When you look at the Apple logo, even without being told, you automatically know that the device carrying the logo was made by Apple – that's the power of branding.

The same way it is important that you develop and stick with a defined color scheme from the get-go, you also need to develop a color scheme for your blog from the beginning. This logo will serve as your favicon and will also appear on your marketing and non-marketing materials. When visitors open your blog or any other of your content, your logo is one of the first things that draw their attention, so you need to dedicate time to develop this critical branding tool.

If you observe the logos of the biggest brands in the world, you will observe one common pattern – their logos are all simple. Take a cue from them and design a simple logo too. You could use Adobe Illustrator or Photoshop to design a logo for yourself.

Adobe allows you to use the software for free for one week, after which you are required pay a subscription fee. You might use the one-week trial period to develop a logo for your blog. However, if you are not versed in graphic designer, you could consider hiring a designer to take care of the job for you. You will find talented designers on freelance websites like Fiverr.com and Upwork.com. When designing your logo, don't forget that your chosen color scheme should be in sync with your logo's color scheme.

Once you are done designing your logo, customizing your logo and getting everything about the blog ready, then it is time to start writing and uploading content to your blog.

Chapter Five:

Populating your blog

with content

After setting up your blog and doing all the necessary customizations, the next thing you want to do is to populate your blog with incisive posts. Earlier, we mentioned that finding the right blog niche is one of the hardest tasks – now, another hard task, when it comes to blogging, is to create and publish valuable posts that your readers would love.

With the right content, the right readers will locate your blog – this will gradually work to help improve the search engine ranking of the blog. Once many of your posts have been ranked on search engines, then you have already come steps closer to running a successful blog. That said, you need to dedicate a lot of time to research and create valuable content –

one that would solve the problems that your readers have.

Your first content

For a first-time blogger, publishing their first content often prove to be a difficult task. The reason is not hard to guess – the blogger usually does not know how and where to find the best topic ideas to share with their readers. Some other new bloggers go ahead to copy contents on other blogs and publish same on theirs. That is a very wrong move as Google would see such content as duplicate and hence would not rank your blog for such contents. Also, copying content from other blogs can make Google penalize your blog, which will make it hard for it to be ranked on the search engine.

Another mistake that new bloggers make is that they just copy posts from blogs, use article rewriters or spinners to change a few common words or phrases in the article. The bloggers do this because they feel they could fool Google to think the content is original.

However, Google still has a way of detecting content that has been spun using article rewriters or article encoding tools. Google sees such articles as duplicate content, and if you have such duplicate content on your blog, you could be penalized.

Now, how do you find topic ideas for your first blog post? There are several available means of finding the right topic ideas for your blog posts – one of them is through social listening.

What is social listening?

Social listening simply involves eavesdropping on the conversations of social media users and picking up useful information which you can use to perform various actions. For instance, when you go on Quora, you will find people asking various questions – what you are doing is social listening.

When you visit a Facebook group, for instance, you will find people discussing various issues – that is a type of social listening. Now, you can use social listening to your advantage – all you need to do is to be proactive instead of reactive. Rather than just listening to what people are saying on social media, provoke them to tell you what problem they want to be solved.

For instance, if you have a blog that talks about Amazon Kindle Publishing and you are looking for a topic idea to publish on your blog, you could visit Quora and ask a question like, "What are the major challenges you are facing as a Kindle Publisher?" You could also ask, "What would you advise a new Kindle Publisher?" You could also ask, "What are the best Amazon Kindle keyword research tools?" You will be surprised to find out that many Quora users would be willing to answer your questions. From their answers, you could grab some pieces of information that will help you create your first blog post.

Apart from Quora, you can also do this type of active social listening on Facebook. Search for Facebook groups that are related to your blog niche. Join such groups and proceed to ask the kind of questions you asked on Quora. You will find many useful answers – especially if you come across as someone who is ready to learn.

For instance, if you asked a question on the best Amazon Kindle keyword research tools, you are likely to get answers like keyword.io, Publisher Rocket, etc. Now, to utilize such information, you can head to your notepad or word process and produce a topic like, "How to find bestselling Amazon Kindle keywords using keyword.io."

Also, if asked a question like, "what are the challenges you face when you run Facebook ads?" You are likely to get answers like, "My major challenge when I run Facebook ads is how to target the right audience." With that answer, you can proceed to create a topic that says, "How to target the right audience when running Facebook ads."

In the above examples, you could see that your conversations with your target audience already revealed the types of problems that they have. With such information on your hands, you don't have to create topics blindly.

While the abovementioned method is suitable for discovering blog post topic ideas, you need not rely on it alone. Once you have gotten a topic idea, you still need to do keyword research to ensure that the problem you want to address is not a solo one. Proper keyword research will show you how many people are seeking a solution to the same problem. If you confirm after keyword research that many people are indeed searching for the topic, then you can proceed and create a blog post around that topic.

Keyword research

As mentioned earlier, keyword research is an important step you must take when creating content for your blog. One mistake that many bloggers make is that they create blog posts for themselves instead of considering their audience. For instance, some bloggers just think about a topic that interests them or one they think their audience would love, then they proceed to create a blog post on such topics. What these bloggers often forget is that they are not the ones reading their own blog.

You are writing for an audience, and sometimes, the topics that your audience wants to read may not be the exact topic that you want. Since you are not necessarily writing for yourself – you should make sure that there are enough people seeking the solution that you want to provide.

Proper keyword research protects you from writing blindly – it shows you the approximate number of people searching for a topic. It also shows you how much advertisers are willing to pay for a specific keyword. All these pieces of information can help you to know if it is worth it spending some time creating a blog post on a given topic.

When we talk of CPC (Cost per Click) or how much advertisers are going to pay for a keyword, it might sound confusing to the new blogger. However, let's try and explain it.

Google and other advertising networks have a way of determining how much you earn when they place advertisements on your blog or web page. CPC is one of the earning models, and there is also CPM (Cost per Impression). Let's proceed further to explain how all these works.

When it comes to the advertisements that Google or other advertising networks place on a website, there are always three parties involved. The first party is you the blog or website owner. The second party is Google or any other ad network like Bing, while the third party is a business owner who wants to advertise their business on relevant websites or blogs.

Typically, a business owner runs an advertisement campaign on Google's advertising network called Google Ads. When setting up the campaign, the business owner states how much they are willing to pay each time someone clicks on their ads. Some high-end businesses bid higher than others, while some businesses bid lower.

Now, once the campaign has been set up, Google advertises the business on your blog or web page. Let's assume that the business agrees they would pay $1.5 for every click. Remember, for the ad to be running on your site, Google has found some keywords that are relevant to the business (running the ad) on your blog. So, we can say that the CPC for the keywords that attracted the ads is $1.5. Each time a visitor to your blog clicks on the ad, the business owner running the ad will pay $1.5 to Google, who will take their cut and pay you the rest.

Normally, some keywords that are related to some high-end businesses have higher CPCs than the others. So, when you are doing keyword research, you should be interested in finding out the search volume for the keyword and the CPC. If the search volume is high, it means the keyword will attract a high amount of traffic to your blog every month. Also, if the CPC is high, it means that with just a few ad clicks, you can earn a substantial amount of money.

Another metric you should look out for when doing keyword research is the competitive score of the keyword. For instance, if the competitive score is 1, it means the keyword is highly competitive, and you may find it hard to rank for such keywords. However, if the competitive score is below 1, it means you can easily rank for the keyword.

Keyword research tools

We have mentioned some of the importance of keyword research - let's proceed to talk about some of the best keyword research tools for bloggers.

1. Soovle

Soovle is a versatile keyword research tool – it scrapes the various search engines on the internet and shows you the search volume and CPC of any keyword you enter. It also shows you different variations of a keyword and how users type the keywords when doing searches on various search engines.

What's more? Soovle is totally free – in fact, it works like a search engine. To use the tool, just type soovle.com into your web browser. On the home page, enter the keyword you want to research into the search bar. As you are typing the keyword, soovle will be scraping the web in real-time and will show you the keyword's CPC and search volume.

Now, if your focus is to rank the keyword on Google, then you will need to concentrate on the Google results. If you want to rank the keyword on Bing, you will need to focus on Bing results.

Apart from showing how many people are searching for a particular keyword on conventional search engines like Google, Bing, Yahoo, and YouTube, Soovle also shows you how your keyword is faring on Amazon.com.

While Soovle is a great keyword research tool, it does not show you all the information you need about a keyword like its competitive score. If you need other pieces of information about a keyword which Soovle cannot show you, then you can make use of any of the other keyword research tools we are going to talk about in this section.

2. Jaaxy.com

This is yet another excellent keyword research tool. Unlike Soovle.com, Jaaxy is a freemium tool – meaning you can use the free version with limited features, but if you want all the features, you will need to pay at least $50/month.

Jaaxy, just like the other keyword research tools, shows you how many people are searching for a keyword in a month. One great feature of Jaaxy that distinguishes it from the other keyword research tools is its QSR (Quoted Search Result) feature – this basically shows you the number of other blogs that are trying to rank for each keyword. Typically, if this number is high, then it means that the competition for the keyword is high. However, if the number is low, it means you can rank on the first page of Google or other search engines for that keyword.

Phrase ∨	link building			History ∨	Q Find Keywords	
Keyword ⓘ		Avg ⓘ	Traffic ⓘ	QSR ⓘ	KQI ⓘ	SEO ⓘ
seo **link building**		961	164	365	Poor	12
backlink **building**		334	57	250	Normal	72
one way **link building**		56	10	216	Great	84
free **link building** tool		256	44	91	Great	96
affordable **link building**		213	37	278	Normal	54

3. Google Keyword Planner

In a previous section of this guide, we talked about Google Keyword Planner. Essentially, the tool owned by Google gives you relevant information about a keyword, so you don't create blog posts blindly.

To use the tool, you must have a Google account, then visit ads.google.com. Use your Google account to log in. On the home page, click on "Tools," then under "planning" click on "keyword planner." Next, click on "discover new keywords," then enter the keyword you want to get information on into the search box.

Your results should look like the screenshot below.

Google Keyword Planner is more robust than the other keyword research tools mentioned earlier. It shows you a lot of information about a keyword that can help you make an informed decision on whether to write on the keyword or not. What's more? The tool is totally free – you only need to have a Gmail account (which is also free) to use it.

Other notable keyword research tools include:

- Keywordtool.io

- Keywords Everywhere – this is a browser extension which we have already talked about in a previous section of this guide.

- Google Trends – we have talked about this tool in a previous section of this guide

- SEMRush.com – a freemium tool that does a great job of helping you find viable keywords

- KWFinder.com

Apart from these mentioned keyword research tools, there are tons of other ones, both free and paid. Do your research and find out the ones that are best for you.

Interpreting results from keyword research

When you conduct research on a keyword, you would be shown the average number of people searching for that keyword in a month. You will also see how competitive the keyword is. Typically, you would think that a keyword with a high search volume is the best – while this is true to some extent, such keywords are often very competitive.

The best keywords are those with high search volume, low to moderate competition, and high CPC. However, finding a keyword that ticks those three boxes can be quite hard. A good idea is for you to compromise on one of the requirements.

For instance, you could go for a keyword with moderate or average search volume, low competition, and high CPC – yes, you can find such keywords. You would want to use your discretion to determine which of the metrics you want to compromise on. For instance, if a keyword has a high search volume, low to moderate competition, and low CPC – you could consider going for the keyword even though the CPC is low because the high search volume will cover up for that.

Additionally, instead of settling for seed keywords, consider their long tails. The long tail of a keyword simply means the expanded forms that can be derived from the root keyword. Each time you type a root or seed keyword into a keyword research tool, you will see a lot of derivatives from that root keyword — those derivatives are called long tails variants of the keyword.

In most cases, the root keyword may not meet your criteria — it might have a high search volume, and the competitive score would be very high as well, so you don't want to use it. However, when you look closely at the long tails of the root keyword, you will find viable variants with an equally good amount of search volume and low competition. You are to go for those long-tail keywords instead of the seed or root keyword.

For instance, if you search for "celery juice," in the results, you will find, "celery juice" as a separate result and you will also find, "benefits of celery juice" as one of the results which could have high good search volume and low competition. Now, instead of just writing a blog post on "celery juice," a smart blogger would write on "benefits of celery juice."

One good thing about making use of long-tail variants of a keyword is that you may end up ranking for both the seed keyword and its long tail variant. When you first publish the post, it will rank for the long tail variant of the keyword. Then after some time, it might rank for the main seed keyword – meaning more traffic to your blog.

Now that you have mastered the art of finding and analyzing good keywords, the next chapter will show you how to write an engaging blog post.

Chapter Six:

How to write an engaging blog post

Before we show you how to write a good blog post – let's, first, analyze the components of such a blog post. Typically, a blog post has three parts – the header or introduction, the body, and the conclusion or calls to action. You need to understand what information should appear in each of these sections if you want to create a high converting and engaging blog post.

The header or introduction

Just as the name implies, the header of your blog post should introduce the idea or topic of the post. It should let the user know what the topic is all about – you can include definitions here if necessary.

Additionally, the header should let the reader know what they are going to gain by reading the blog post to the end. It is important that you use emotional triggers to keep the reader hooked and feel they would miss something important if they do not read to the end.

For instance, if you are writing a blog post on the benefits of childproofing your home, you could start by defining what home childproofing means. You could proceed to let the reader know that in addition to learning the benefits of childproofing their home, they are also going to learn the top five ways to childproof their home. This way, you have piqued the reader's interest, and they would want to read your post to the very end.

The body

The main body of your blog post comes immediately after the header, and it is where you present your main argument. For ease of readability, you could consider presenting your points in the form of a listicle. You should also use subheadings or subtitles to separate one main point from the other to make it easier for the reader to scan through your points.

As we have always been reiterating, you are not creating a blog post for yourself – instead, you are doing it for your readers. So, you should present your readers with valuable information in a readable format so that in the end, they could feel you have helped them so that they could continue reading your other posts for more information.

Conclusion and call to action

You should use the concluding part of your post to chip in some pieces of information that you did not cover in the main body of the post. Don't start repeating all the points you have already treated in the body of the post – that would be an unnecessary repetition. After concluding the post, include a call-to-action to tell the reader what to do next.

Call-to-action is an integral part of every blog post – your average reader may know the next action to take after reading your post, but they still expect you to tell them what to do. This is your chance to make them take the desired action. Before even writing a post, you should have figured out the goal you want to achieve with the post. You are to use a call-to-action to accomplish this goal.

For instance, if you want the reader to comment, let them know using a call-to-action. If you want them to join your email list, read other related articles, download an eBook, or share your article, let them know. As mentioned earlier, do not assume that the reader knows what to do next – they may know, but they still want you to tell them. The average blog would click away after reading your post if you do not tell them the next thing to do.

SEO articles and blog posts

Search Engine Optimization simply involves crafting posts so that they can be easily ranked by search engines such as Google, Bing, etc. When it comes to SEO, some articles are often referred to as SEO articles, while others are not. The major difference is that SEO articles or blog posts contain relevant keywords in strategic sections of the article like the header, body, and conclusion.

When you are writing a blog post, it is important that optimization is done for search engine ranking – this way, your ideal reader can discover and read the article. Optimizing your posts for search engine ranking is very important because, without it, your posts will be undiscoverable. What is the point of writing a blog post if it won't be discovered and read by your target audience?

Before writing a blog post, make sure you have used any of the keyword research tools we discussed in the previous section to analyze the keyword. After your analysis, write out at least three keywords which you would include in different parts of your article. Ideally, you should include keywords in the title, header, body, and conclusion of your blog post.

Ensure you don't stuff keywords unnecessarily in your blog post as that could attract a penalty. Keyword stuffing will also alter the natural flow of your blog and make it nearly unreadable. For clarity, keyword stuffing is the act of including an excessive number of keywords at different places in your blog post. People who do keyword stuffing think it is a good way of adding as many keywords as possible in their posts to improve ranking.

Most times, instead of improving the search engine ranking of your blog post, keyword stuffing works to reduce its readability and conversion rate. Rather than stuffing unnecessary keywords in your blog post, take your take and learn the proper way of incorporating the right number of keywords in the blog post – this will help improve the readability of your article and increase your conversion rate.

Writing an engaging blog post

The average internet user is not the most patient person out there – they also have a short attention span. This means that if you want them to read your posts, you must make them as highly engaging as possible.

Here are some of the ways to write an engaging blog post:

1. Write in a conversational style

When you are creating a blog post, you should focus on the person who will read the post – you can do that by writing in a conversational style. Such style of writing will increase your post engagement by up to 80%.

Think about this – a lecturer walks into a classroom filled with students, starts talking without even referring to the students, what do you think the students would do? Many of them would fall asleep because the lecture must be boring to endure. However, if the lecturer enters the classroom and creates a conversation where everyone in the class contributes and feels among, what do you think would happen? The class would be lively.

The best way to write in a conversational style is to use "I" and "You" in your posts. Using those two words makes your posts personalized to the reader – the reader would feel you are talking to them directly. It is also an excellent way to create dialogue and encourage more of your readers to engage with your posts.

You can say things like, "I am happy you are reading this post," "thank you for being here," "in this article, I am going to show you…"

Any reader who comes across any of the above phrases would feel you are talking to them directly and would want to continue reading. Without writing in a conversational style, your post will sound like an academic thesis or a research document, and no one loves reading those kinds of materials except when it is extremely necessary.

2. Break down your content into many paragraphs

When people open your blog post and find it to be one huge chunk of text, they will not hesitate to close the page and go elsewhere. You need to group your points into paragraphs, and each paragraph should contain about four sentences or 4 lines. Once a paragraph starts getting long, create a new one. It is also a good idea to present your ideas using a list – this improves readability significantly.

3. Make sure you use subheadings

If your blog post is such a long one – ensure you use subheadings to highlight your major points. Even if your content is not that long, you can still make use of subheadings. Subheadings help to improve the readability of your post because someone could just skim through and grab the main points of your post.

4. Throw in images to spice up things

Whenever possible, throw in relevant pictures to lighten up your posts and spice things up a little. Many times, when people open a blog post, they scan through for images – they want to draw conclusions from the pictures or use them to understand what the post is all about. Something as simple as a crisp, welcoming image is enough to keep your reader glued to your post. Additionally, well-labeled images help with search engine optimization.

You can follow the above tips and write as many posts as possible for your new blog until you have totally populated the blog.

In the next chapter, we shall start looking at different ways of monetizing your blog.

Chapter Seven:

SEO (Search Engine Optimization)

Search Engine Optimization (SEO) involves designing your blog and modifying its contents so that search engines can easily index and rank the blog. If your blog is ranked on search engines, it means that potential readers who search for keywords related to the ones you have on your blog will find your blog and proceed to visit and read the content you have on there.

It is safe to say that SEO is a way of tricking Google to show your blog or articles to potential readers when these people do online searches. In the world of blogging and internet marketing as a whole, SEO is very important, and SEO strategies change from time to time, which is why bloggers are always on the lookout for new SEO strategies.

The average blog reader relies on Google to lead them to the information they seek. If your blog is ranked on Google so that the average blog reader could find it when doing searches, you will have consistent traffic to your blog. If you cannot optimize your blog for the search engines, then your traffic will suffer. Unless you run a popular blog that everybody already knows, then SEO is your best hope of getting consistent traffic.

Because SEO strategies take time to yield results, some people think SEO is no longer relevant – however, the truth remains that SEO is still as effective as it has always been. As a newbie blogger without much financial strength to run social media and other types of online ads, then SEO is your only hope. However, you must do it right; otherwise, it would turn back and hurt your blog.

Some careless SEO strategies could make Google penalize your blog. Some other SEO strategies could lead to the suspension of your AdSense account – so, while you are trying hard to make your blog search engine optimized, you need to make sure that you are adopting the right SEO strategies.

Every day, Google and the other search engines change their search algorithms – these changes are always accompanied by a change in SEO practices. In other words, the world of SEO is an ever-changing one; what is in vogue today may get outdated the next moment, and that's the reason the topic of SEO is always on every blogger's lips.

Many times, new bloggers ask some questions concerning SEO such as, "what is SEO," "what are the best strategies when it comes to SEO for blogs," "where can one outsource SEO services?" amidst other questions. Responding to the subject of the best SEO practices or strategies for blogs can be very tricky because as we said earlier, SEO strategies are always changing.

But despite the constant changes, the core basics of SEO remain the same. When we say that the core basics have remained the same, we mean that even though some strategies might have changed, there are still things about SEO that have remained relatively the same. In this chapter, we shall not be teaching you specific ways to do SEO – instead, we shall be concentrating on showing you the current SEO best strategies.

The best SEO is to stay focused on the visitor

The mistake that most people make when it comes to SEO is trying out different strategies all the time. Over the years, it has proven not to be the best approach to SEO. Instead of running around and testing out different SEO techniques or tricks, it would be better if you focus on one basic concept that states that the best SEO is the one that is human based.

Saying that the best SEO is human-based SEO can be surprising to many because they have long thought that the best techniques involve outsourcing SEO services to SEO consultants, or using automation tools, binary code, or shortcuts. While many of these techniques might have worked some years back when they were in vogue, they no longer stand the chance of being regarded as the best SEO practices today.

In today's SEO circle, the best strategies revolve around knowing who your blog readers are, connecting with them personally, and assisting them to solve their problems. Blog visitors are people looking for solutions to their problems, and if you understand it this way and provide them with a solution to their problem, then you have the best SEO strategy.

The algorithm that search engines use to rank websites might have changed several times over the years, but one single thing remains constant, and that constant thing is that every search engine is out to provide useful content that will serve the needs of website visitors.

Today, we might be talking more about the demand for performance, mobile inquiries, and long voice-based search phrases, yet one thing remains constant – the needs of the visitor must be met. So, as long as humans are the ones visiting blogs, the need for high-quality human-based SEO will always be there. Providing tangible value and placing a strong focus on user experience will always be the best SEO strategy.

Don't be too engrossed thinking about plugins, data, and website code as the real SEO. Yes, all these may come into play in ranking a blog, but the most essential thing that you must not ignore is to provide the blog visitor with the best user experience so that they don't find it difficult getting the solution they seek on your blog.

You need to understand that following shortcuts or outsourcing SEO services to acclaimed consultants may not really do much for you. The most important thing is the real value and experience you give your visitors. Following shortcuts or outsourcing your SEO services may bring visitors to your blog, but these shortcuts won't connect with these visitors on a personal level. Remember that the people visiting your website are real humans seeking solutions to their pains, and you need to address them as real humans.

SEO is complex and yet so simple

The world of SEO is an ever-changing one; everything seems to be getting more and more complex. Long search phrases are now the order of the day. Longer articles are also becoming the standard, and search engines are not left out as they have developed complex algorithms to be able to process all the changes that are taking place. Yet, amidst all these changes, we can say that things haven't changed much.

Search engines are still looking for websites and blogs that provide value to the visitors. So, Google expects that you do the right thing, and the right thing here involves providing value to people every day.

Many times, people want to know if they could game the system and make use of code or automation tools to push their blogs to the top of search engine result pages. The truth is that using these automation tools and codes might have worked in the past, but they no longer work today. If your focus is only on getting your blog way up the search engine result pages, then it clearly means that you have lost focus on the visitor, and once it is not about the visitor, it is not the best SEO.

Human-based SEO is about helping people solve their problems, and you need to know that black hat tricks don't help blog readers to solve their problems. At best, they help you get your blog to the top of the search result, but Google has developed a quick way of removing the websites and blogs that game their system.

The bottom line is that you need to take time to learn about SEO in-depth, especially if you are new to it. Don't opt for shortcuts, don't bother yourself about changing algorithms; just learn the basics. Try to understand why people visit and stay on websites, as that will help you reach your goals.

Your focus should always be on your visitors, their unique problems, and how you can help them solve these problems. SEO strategies may be changing, but the core SEO principles remain the same – which is to serve the visitor.

Here are a few things you should do to improve your search engine ranking:

1. Improve your site speed

The average blog reader has only a few seconds to wait for your blog to load. If your blog doesn't load within those few seconds, then the visitor would be forced to leave. Since Google and other search engines always put the experience of the website visitor first, it means that if your blog loads fast enough, your search engine ranking will be improved.

2. Reduce bounce rate

Bounce rate and site speed go hand in hand – the reason is simple – if your blog is slow to load, your bounce rate will be high. With a high bounce rate, Google would be forced to believe that your site does not have what the visitor is searching for, and this would impact your ranking negatively.

Even though site speed is not the only thing that affects the bounce rate of your blog, it remains one of the major causes. Other things that could cause an increase in your bounce rate include a poorly designed blog. If your visitors find it hard to navigate through your blog easily, they would be forced to leave, thus increasing your bounce rate.

Additionally, make sure your blog posts contain value and provide a solution to the problem the reader has. These days, Google and the other search engines prefer longer articles to shorter ones. This is not implying that you should use filler content to make up your post. Instead, ensure you cover every necessary point so that the reader could say, "Yes, I got value."

Furthermore, if you don't write in a conversational style, you could also chase away visitors, and this affects your bounce rate. If you don't know how to make use of calls-to-action creatively, then you could be increasing your blog's bounce rate. With the right call-to-action, you could direct visitors to other relevant and related articles on your blog. This way, they could go on a reading spree instead of bouncing off after reading the first article.

As mentioned earlier, these days, learning all the SEO tricks and strategies in the world will not help you. Yes, you still need to know some fundamental SEO strategies like writing search engine optimized articles, but if your blog eventually gets ranked and you don't retain visitors, you may end up losing your ranking.

So, it is more important to ensure that your blog provides value. Start by improving your site speed and provide useful content. If you do all this, your bounce rate will decrease, and Google would be forced to believe that your blog is valuable; hence, your ranking will improve.

Chapter Eight:
Blog monetization

If you have followed this guide religiously, then at this point, you must have found a blog niche, decided on the best blogging platform, designed your blog, written and uploaded posts on your blog.

Now, if you have done all that, the next thing to do is to monetize your blog and earn money from your efforts. In the past, people used to start blogs just to document their life or merely for the joy of it. Today, people consider blogs as a viable online business which can give them money while they are doing the things they love.

In a previous section of this guide, we talked about some of the ways of monetizing a blog. In this section, we are going to spend time talking about the Google AdSense program, which is one of the most popular blog monetization methods out there.

What is Google AdSense?

Google AdSense is one of Google's integrated services that gives website owners and bloggers the chance to place ads on their website and earn money when visitors click on those ads.

How the program works is: an advertiser approaches Google, create an ad campaign – then Google looks for a website that is registered in the AdSense program and places those ads on the site. Google goes through every website and ensures that the ads they are putting on it are relevant to the visitors of the website.

Google also considers the type of content that a website has when placing ads. For instance, if you run a travel blog, most of the ads that Google would push to your site would be those related to travel. It could be the ads of travel companies, airlines, flight agents, etc.

When visitors come to your website and click on any of the Google ads placed at strategic sections on your website or blog, Google analyses the click action to verify that it is valid. If Google confirms that the click action is legitimate, it pays you according to the amount that the advertiser agreed with Google (CPC). If, on the other hand, Google discovers that a click action on an ad placed on your blog is invalid; that could lead to a suspension of your Google AdSense account.

Who is free to join the Google AdSense program?

Ideally, anyone who has a blog or website (that doesn't have adult content or promote betting/gambling) can apply and get approved for the Google AdSense program. However, for some reasons, some people do not get their application approved. If you visit online forums, you will find people complaining that their AdSense application was declined.

There are several reasons that could make Google decline one's application to join the AdSense program. Also, there are a few things you need to put in place before applying for Google AdSense. With those things in place, your application would be approved on your first try.

Why do many people prefer Google AdSense to other online ad networks?

Before we proceed to talk about some of the things you need to put in place before applying for Google AdSense program, let's quickly why many people prefer AdSense. Often people ask, "Why do so many people prefer the Google AdSense program to other similar programs?"

The answer to that question is – while there are other online ad networks out there, the fact remains that Google AdSense is the most popular. Because of the popularity of Google and their integrated services, many advertisers naturally pitch their tent with Google when they want to advertise on online platforms. Also, Google pays better than many of the other ad networks. Some other ad networks don't have a transparent payment policy, unlike Google, that makes sure you receive what you have earned as long as the click that earned you that income is valid.

Now, let's proceed to talk about how to get AdSense approval on your first try. It is important that you get your AdSense application approved on your first try because if you fail the first time, your chances of failing to secure the approval on your second try are high. Once you have tried the first time and failed, Google kind of places your domain name on a watch list (this is an unwritten rule or code). So, you want to do everything possible to get approved on your first try.

Getting Google AdSense approval is not as hard as many people make it seem. The truth is that if you follow all the steps and do the right things, Google would have no other option than to approve your website for AdSense. If you have followed all the steps outlined in this book so far, then you should not have a problem getting AdSense approval.

That said, here are the things you need to put in order before applying for AdSense approval:

1. A decent blog site

Whether you are using the Blogger platform or WordPress, it doesn't matter when it comes to AdSense approval; Google cares more about the functionality of your website. The blog site has to be well designed so that it is attractive to visitors. Google takes the experience of the blog visitor seriously – they want to make sure that your blog visitor gets the best experience when they visit your blog.

Having a good theme can do a lot for your blog in terms of design. You are better off with a premium theme than a free one. Premium themes have better features, and you can customize your blog to look as stunning as possible.

Now one way to make your blog appealing to both your visitors and Google is to improve its speed. Google hates blogs with low speed – the reason is simple – low speed means high bounce rate, and with high bounce rate, ads would not be clicked, and if the ads are not accessed, both you and Google will not earn.

On the other hand, if your blog loads fast enough, the visitor would be pleased to read as many posts on your blog as possible. While reading posts, they could be prompted to click on ads – therefore Google prefers websites that load faster.

In addition to aiding AdSense approval, website speed also impacts SEO. In the past, Google used to rank only blogs that contain the keywords that the reader is searching for. Today, however, Google looks beyond keywords and considers other factors like site speed when ranking blogs and websites.

So, even if you write the best search engine optimized articles, blog posts and your blog crawls like a snail in terms of speed, you would find it hard to rank on the first page of Google and the other search engines.

In addition to ensuring that your blog loads fast, you need to make sure you include clear navigation on your blog. Google prefers those blogs that have the elements of a proper website – all this still boils down to giving the visitor the best experience.

Typically, Google wants you to include an "About Page," "Contact Page," and a "Privacy Policy Page" on your blog before applying for AdSense approval. Adding all these pages to your blog should not be a huge task – you simply need to create a new page, name it "About Us" for instance and include what the reader needs to know about you. Google wants you to treat your blog as a business – that's why it is forcing you to include an "About Us" section.

Your "Contact Us" page should contain basic information on how your blog readers can contact you. You could include your phone number, email, or a contact form so that your blog readers can get in touch with you. If you have a physical address for your business, you can include it in this section; otherwise, you are good with just adding your phone number and email.

The "privacy policy page" is the one that Google takes more seriously – in fact, Google may still approve your site if you don't have "About Us" and "Contact Us" pages but if you don't have a "Privacy Policy" page, then your chances of approval are almost non-existent.

When creating your privacy policy page, there are specific pieces of information that Google wants you to include. This article from Google shows you the information you must include. If you are finding it hard to string together a privacy policy page, then consider using this free privacy policy generator.

Additionally, a good logo will contribute to making your blog look as professional as possible. We have already mentioned that severally in the previous sections of this guide. If you have not gotten a logo yet, then endeavor to get one as it will improve your chances of getting approved for AdSense.

2. Quality content

In addition to having a decent website, quality content is another thing that Google considers before approving AdSense application. They want to be sure that the contents you are putting up on your blog are those that can solve the problem of the reader. As mentioned earlier, Google values the experience of the reader more than anything else, and they want to ensure that, at every point, the user gets a pleasant experience. The internet giant,

Google knows that if the user gets a good experience when visiting a blog, then the user will be more likely to click on ads.

So, to increase your chances of getting AdSense approval, you must create useful, articulate, and original content. You cannot just throw up some spammy content you copied from other websites and expect Google to approve your application. Remember, Google places a premium on user experience, and since spam content irritates the average user, Google would never approve any blog containing such contents for AdSense. Posting spam content on your blog will also affect your search engine ranking negatively – so, you need to avoid it entirely.

Google wants you to solve the problem that people have – if they find that your blog is solving problems, then they will approve it for AdSense. How do you solve people's problem? Through keyword research. After doing keyword research, take the time to write an original, articulate post that addresses the issue you have identified. Make sure you intersperse the post with relevant keywords to improve its search engine ranking.

One mistake that many new and even old bloggers make is that they go on eZinearticles.com, copy articles and post the same on their blog, then apply for AdSense and expect to get approved. Some even create auto blogs and fill it with copied contents and expect Google to approve the site for monetization. If you do that, then you should not be surprised if Google turns down your application. It is good to put yourself in the position of your blog reader – if you were the one reading your own blog, would you be happy to read some of the contents you have put up there? Your answer to that question should guide you.

Ideally, before you apply for AdSense approval, make sure you have posted up to 10 well-written articles. Each article should be up to 1,000 words in length. Make sure you do proper keyword research before writing the articles. Once you have gotten up to the recommended ten (10), don't just jump right in and apply for AdSense. You need to wait for some time and allow the articles to rank on search engine – this will increase the amount of traffic coming to your blog. Note: Google also considers the traffic coming to a blog before approving AdSense for the blog.

Overall, to get AdSense approval, you want to:

- Make sure you have a well-designed blog with all the necessary pages
- Make sure you are posting original search engine optimized articles

Quick tip! If your blog is in one of those popular, saturated niches such as making money online, marketing, SEO, etc. then you may find it hard to get AdSense approval. This is one of the reasons why you need to niche down when finding a niche.

Also, you need to wait for at least three months before applying for AdSense. If you just create a blog today, populate it with articles the next day and apply for AdSense the following week, your application will likely not get approved. Also, you need to have a custom domain name to increase your chances of getting approved. Using a subdomain sends a signal that you are not serious.

Applying for Google AdSense

Once you have gotten all the requirements, the next step is to apply for Google AdSense and await your approval. If you have followed all the tips mentioned above, then there is a high chance that your application will be approved on your first try.

To apply for Google AdSense, follow this link. You will be asked to provide your blog URL, your name, contact information, email address, phone number, mailing address, and a few other basic pieces of information. At this initial stage of the application, you will not be required to submit your bank account information or TIN – that will be later when your application has been approved.

Important: make sure that the mailing address and indeed, all the personal information you are providing is correct. A PIN will be sent to your mailing address for verification purposes – so, if you input a wrong address, you will fail the address verification. Also, you will be required to verify your phone number – although these verifications will not happen until a later time, you need to get everything right from the beginning.

Filling out the application is not hard – you just need to follow the prompts – you only need to provide basic information about you and your blog. You will only spend a few minutes filling out the forms.

Getting approved to place temporary ads

After submitting your application, the Google AdSense team will review it to see if your blog should be accepted into the AdSense program. Typically, the approval occurs within 24 to 48 hours after application. If you have followed all the steps and tips in this guide, then getting approval should be the least of your worries.

If you are approved, Google will send you an email that you have passed the first stage of the process. The email will further explain the other processes you need to go through until you are fully verified. At this first stage, what Google does is that they temporarily approve your blog to run ads and after you earn a certain amount of money from clicks on, you are prompted to do an address verification.

At this point, you will be shown how to place ads on your blog – you will also be able to login to your AdSense account and see how much you have earned from clicks on the ads you have placed on your blog.

From the time you are approved to place ads on your blog temporarily, Google will be monitoring your activities to ensure you are not clicking on your own ads, sending traffic from suspicious sources to your blog, or using tricks to increase clicks on your ads. As long as you are not clicking on your ads, sending friends to click on the ads, or using tricks or bots to click on your ads, you should be fine.

If you log into your AdSense dashboard, you will find where Google places AdSense codes which you can copy and put on your blog. Those codes are what will display as ads when viewers view them on their browser.

To increase your earnings, place different AdSense codes on strategic sections of your blog where readers can see and click them. However, do remember that the average internet user hates to see ads, so you should know where you are placing ads – you don't want to choke your readers with them.

If you have two or more blogs, you can place your AdSense codes on those blogs and increase your earnings. You don't have to apply individually for each new blog – you simply need to create new ad units and color themes for your different blogs. You are creating a new ad unit and color theme because you want the displayed ad to match the theme of each of your blog or website.

AdSense verification

Once your AdSense application has been approved, you can start generating ad units, place the ad codes on your blog, and earn money from clicks. Once you reach a certain threshold, Google will need to verify your physical address, bank account, phone number, and tax information. Without verifying these details, Google will not pay you what you have earned from AdSense.

To start the verification process, log into your AdSense dashboard, you will see a button that will prompt you to begin the verification process. When you click the button, Google will mail a PIN to the physical address you provided. The mail will get to you after seven to ten days. The mail you receive will contain your verification PIN. You will need to log into your dashboard and enter the PIN you received via mail to complete your address verification.

The mail will look like the screenshot below.

Your Google AdSense Personal Identification Number (PIN)

Welcome to Google AdSense. To enable payment for your account, we kindly ask that you follow these 4 simple steps:

STEP 1: Log in to your AdSense account at www.google.com/adsense/ with the email address and password you used during the application process.
STEP 2: From the **Home** tab, click **Account settings** in the left navigation bar.
STEP 3: In the **Account Information** section, click on the "**verify address**" link.
STEP 4: Enter your PIN as it appears below and click **Submit PIN**.

Your PIN: ▮▮▮▮▮▮

If you have additional questions, please visit the AdSense Help Center at www.google.com/adsense/support/as. Our payments guide can be found at www.google.com/adsense/payments.

Thanks,
The Google AdSense Team

Apart from the PIN verification, you may be required to verify your bank account information, but that usually comes later. When verifying your bank account information, you will be required to fill out your tax information. One of the requirements for the bank verification is that the name you applied with must be the same as your bank account name. If you applied with your business entity, the bank account name must be the same as your business entity.

If you want to get paid by ACH (which is the preferred option), you will need to provide your bank account number and routing number. Google will deposit a small amount into the bank account and withdraw it afterward. As part of the verification, you will be asked to input this small amount into your Google AdSense dashboard. If you enter the correct amount that was deposited into your bank account, then your bank account verification has become completed. You can then start getting paid monthly as long as you reach the minimum withdrawal limit.

If you did not verify your phone when you were filling out your application, you would be asked to do so. Google will send a code to your phone number, which you will input into your dashboard or place an automated call with your verification code to you. Once you input the verification code, then you are good to go.

How to keep your AdSense account safe

Getting your AdSense account approved and verified does not mean that the account cannot be banned later if you do not follow AdSense's terms and conditions. One common factor that could lead to the banning of your account is invalid clicks.

If you don't click on your ads and you don't recruit people to click on the ads, then you are safe. Also, if you do not use bots or click farms to click on the ads, then you are also safe. If you don't place your ad codes on pornographic sites, then you are also safe.

Publishing copyrighted material on your blog can also lead to the termination of your account. The owner of the copyrighted material could report your blog to Google, and this could lead to an account ban.

One of the reasons why you need to avoid an AdSense account ban, by all means, is that once you have been banned, you cannot place AdSense codes on all the blogs and websites linked with the banned account. So, even if you get a new AdSense account, you will still not be able to generate ad codes and place on your previous blogs. You will need to start building and growing an entire blog from scratch – this can take a long time.

The best way to avoid the termination of your account is to read AdSense's terms and conditions carefully – once you follow those terms, then you will have your account all to yourself as long as you want.

How to earn more with your ads

Some of the obvious ways to earn more money from ads include:

- Research and create posts on keywords with high CPC
- Find keywords with high search volume

Of course, while the two methods above can help you earn more from your blog, there are ways you could play around or be smart with your ads and increase your earnings. For instance, you could do manual tests and ad placements to determine the best sections on your blog to place ads for maximum conversion. If you place ads on certain areas of your blog, your readers may not get to see and click on them. So, you need to do an A/B split test to determine the best sections for ads clicks.

To do proper A/B split test, you need to place ads in one section or location on your blog, then record the number of people that will click on the ad in one or two days. After a day or two, place the ad codes on entirely different sections of your blog and watch its performance over a day or two. Use your AdSense dashboard to monitor how your ads performed across different locations and sections.

Once you have determined the best places where your ads perform better, then stick to placing your ads in those locations. For some time, their ads convert better when placed on the sidebars. For others, their ads perform better when placed in horizontally in between two posts. For some others, their ads perform better when they place them in between the content of a post. Conducting a proper A/B split test will help you to determine your own ad conversion hotspot.

Can I Use other monetization methods apart from AdSense?

There are obviously tons of other blog monetization programs like AdSense, which you can use on your blog. If you want to use those other monetization methods alongside AdSense, then you need to be careful and ensure you are not about to spam your blog with lots of ads which could give your readers a bad experience.

Even though Google does not frown at using other monetization methods alongside AdSense, having a competitor monetization program before applying for AdSense could cause Google not to approve your application. There is no official word from Google that affirms this – however, the experiences of other bloggers have shown that many times, Google rarely approves AdSense accounts for blogs that already have other similar monetization programs in place.

When your account has been approved, you can place ads from other networks alongside AdSense, but you need to consider the interest of the reader first and ensure you are not bombarding them with ads.

Note: those other AdSense alternatives are obviously not as popular as AdSense. Also, some of them are not as transparent as AdSense when it comes to payment of amount earned. Furthermore, while AdSense has a stringent approval process, some of the alternatives even have a more stringent process. So, getting approved into some of the programs is even harder than getting into AdSense.

That being said, here are some of the popular AdSense alternatives:

- AdThrive – you will need to have gotten up to 100k pageviews all-time to be accepted by AdThrive.
- Media Vine – this ad network requires that you have up to 50k views all-time to join their program.
- Ezoic

Note: many of these mentioned ad networks still work with Google to serve ads on your blog. So, most of them are still connected to Google in one way or the other. Unlike AdSense, most of them pay you per 1000 visits. They have a specific amount they pay you for every 1,000 visits that your blog records. If you get a lot of traffic to your blog, then you may earn more with these AdSense alternatives than with AdSense itself.

The only downside is that they require that your blog has a lot of traffic before you can apply. Another downside is that some of them don't have a transparent analytics system with which you can track the performance of their ads on your blog.

Apart from placing pay per click ads and other forms of online or display ads on your blog, you can also earn money with your blog via affiliate programs – Amazon affiliate program and many others are available to bloggers. We shall talk about the Amazon affiliate program in a subsequent section of this guide.

In this chapter, we have been looking at blog monetization using AdSense. We have seen that placing AdSense ads on your site is one of the best ways of monetizing your blog. We have also seen that getting your AdSense account approved is not rocket science – if you follow the steps in this guide, you will get your account approved on your first try.

In the next chapter of this guide, we shall look at other blog monetization methods.

Chapter Nine: Blog monetization – Sponsorships

Apart from placing pay per click (PPC) ads on your blog, you could also consider charging brands to publish their posts on your blog – however, you must let your readers know that such posts are sponsored. This is one of the advantages of running a niche blog – you can publish sponsored posts for companies that sell items related to what you blog about.

For instance, if you blog about mobile devices, phone companies can pay you money to publish phone reviews on your blog. The sponsor will pay depending on how many weeks, days, or months they want the sponsored post to stay up on your blog. The amount you get paid also depends on the traffic that gets to your blog. Typically, if you have huge traffic, you can charge more.

How do you find sponsors?

There are two possible ways to secure sponsorships for your blog – you could let the sponsors come to you, and you can also get proactive and pitch to them. While the former method is suitable, it means you would be leaving your earning potential to chance. With the latter method, you are essentially taking the bull by the horns and reaching out to potential sponsors.

The internet has made the world a very small village indeed – today; companies understand that inbound marketing methods that involve circulating contents about their business on as many platforms as possible are one of the best ways of attracting customers. Hence, you will find companies that scout the internet looking for where to post guest content about their business.

Once your blog starts getting a lot of traffic, you will be surprised to discover the number of businesses that will contact you to post guest articles for them. As mentioned earlier, these businesses search through the internet looking for high traffic blogs where they could advertise their business.

If your blog catches the interest of a potential sponsor, they would get in touch with you and seal a guest posting deal. Sometimes, the business could demand that you post and pin an article they would supply you in specific locations on your blog. Your agreement with the sponsor will detail how many days, weeks, or months that their guest post would stay up on your blog.

While it is great to anticipate businesses to contact you for sponsorship, it is better that you create a sponsored or guest post policy. You can do this by creating a page or section on your blog where you detail your criteria for accepting sponsored or guest posts. Make sure you create a navigation link to this page or section, and the label of the navigation link should read something like, "We accept guest posts."

You could also create a sidebar or banner with the text, "to advertise on this blog, click here." Businesses in your niche that want to advertise on your blog through sponsored or guest posts will contact you, so you negotiate a deal.

If your blog has a lot of traffic and you know how to close deals, you can rest assured that accepting guest or sponsored posts could give you consistent income. If you are running a niche blog, there will always be a business willing to advertise related products or services on your blog.

One important rule you must follow when posting guest or sponsored content is to let the reader know that what you posted is sponsored content. You could get sued if you pass off the sponsored article as organic content. Also, Google could penalize your blog if you are not upfront with your readers about such articles.

Overall, sponsored posts are a great way to earn money on your blog, but you must be upfront with your readers about such posts. Not being upfront about such means you could be misleading your audience, and that could attract serious consequences.

Chapter Ten:
Blog monetization – Amazon affiliate program

In the previous chapter, we mentioned selling ad space as one of the ways of making money with your blog. In this chapter, we shall look at another blog monetization method, which is affiliate marketing. There are many types of affiliate marketing programs; we shall be focusing on Amazon affiliate marketing program. This is a form of an affiliate marketing program where you promote Amazon products on your blog such that when someone buys the product through your efforts, you earn a commission. Before we go deeply into Amazon affiliate marketing, let's, first, define what affiliate marketing is.

What is affiliate marketing?

In simple terms, affiliate marketing is a business model that involves promoting other people's products and earn a commission. Essentially, what you do as an affiliate marketer is: you look for companies that have affiliate programs, register with them, promote their products, and if any sales occur through your efforts, you earn a commission.

To promote a product, you will be given what is called an affiliate link – this link is used to track all the purchases that happened as a result of your marketing efforts. You can get an affiliate link from the company or service provider running the affiliate program.

There are different types of affiliate programs – more and more companies today have recognized affiliate marketing as a viable means of promoting and selling their products; hence, most of them have their own affiliate programs.

An affiliate program is an organized program developed by companies which allow interested persons to market the products of the company and earn a commission. As mentioned earlier, most of the standard companies you use today and most service providers you will be using as a blogger have their own affiliate programs. So, if you could promote the services of these companies to your blog readers, then you can earn a commission.

Affiliate marketing is an excellent way of earning money with your blog – the income from affiliate marketing is passive. Also, you do not need to develop a product or create a service. Other people have already done that for you, all you need do is to promote an existing product and earn a commission. The keyword here is "promote," not "sell." You are essentially telling your readers about a product; then it is then up to them to decide to buy or not.

Affiliate marketing is a win-win for both you, the company running the program and the customer. It is a win for you because you do not have to stress yourself to develop a product or service – you can promote an existing product.

It is a win for the company running the affiliate program because it is a cheaper way for them to market their products and services and gain new customers. Lastly, it is a win for the customer because the products or services you refer to them can help solve their problems.

If you have grown a massive audience of blog readers, then you need to make money off this audience by promoting affiliate products to them. No matter your blog niche, there will always be an affiliate product or service you can promote to your readers. For instance, if you blog about fishing, you could promote fishing equipment like rods, nets, etc. to your readers. Ideally, someone who is interested in fishing would also love to buy fishing equipment, and if they buy through your affiliate link, you make money.

Affiliate marketing did not start today

You may have been doing affiliate marketing for free without knowing it. If you have ever visited a new restaurant down the road, you liked their food, and you talked to your friend and said, "Hey, have you visited that new restaurant? They make some nice delicacies." That's some form of affiliate marketing, even though the eatery did not pay you for it.

Since you have probably done affiliate marketing without pay in the past, then why not consider doing the paid one? It is as simple as joining an affiliate program, get affiliate links, write a few things about the product and publish on a section of your blog, and earn a commission when one of your blog readers purchases the product through your affiliate link.

Amazon affiliate program

As mentioned earlier, there are tons of affiliate programs that you can join and make money. One of the most popular is Amazon affiliate program. Amazon affiliate program was developed to help bloggers and website owners like you to earn a commission on sales made on Amazon.

Amazon is still one of the largest e-commerce marketplaces, and millions of people shop on the platform daily. Also, billions of transactions take place on the site daily. Amazon has already developed a solid brand, so it is not your job to convince your readers on the credibility of Amazon – their strong brand identity already speaks for them. Your only job is to promote their products and earn a commission.

So, how that would work is: on your blog, you have to create a post about a product or a book that is sold on Amazon, you can use a special affiliate link that Amazon will give you to track everybody that visits Amazon and makes a purchase through you. By that tracking, anything that the person buys on Amazon in a 24-hour period would actually be referred back to you so that you can earn a commission. The range of commission you receive varies from 4 to 7% of the price of the product.

Why beginners should join the Amazon affiliate program

There are thousands of affiliate programs and affiliate marketing networks out there that you could start with; however, beginners are often advised to start their affiliate marketing journey with Amazon affiliate program for so many reasons including the ones below:

1. It is easier

If you want to start with the other affiliate marketing networks or programs, you need to have strong salesmanship skills. You need to know how to sell and take people through being a cold lead to a warm buyer.

With Amazon.com affiliate program, you don't need to do that. Amazon is a global brand, and they have perfected their website to the extent that simply visiting the site gets people into a buying mode. This means that most times when people visit the website, there must be something for them to buy. So, your only job will be to send traffic to the site and make money if they make a purchase.

2. There are unlimited products to promote

The products and niches on Amazon keep increasing every day. In fact, thousands of new products are added to the website every single day. If one product or niche becomes saturated, there are thousands of new hot selling products that you can promote and make money. And you can always find something related to your niche which you can promote.

3. You can make money from the sales of products you didn't pitch

You can make a lot of money selling products that you have not pitched. For instance, let's say your niche is audio equipment. And you do review all kinds of microphones and recommend them to people. What happens is, if you refer someone to Amazon, and perhaps, the person gets to Amazon.com, changes their mind and decides to buy a TV set instead, as long as the purchase was made within 24 hours from the time you referred the customer to Amazon, you will still earn commission, even if they didn't buy the original product that you pitched to them.

How to join

Joining Amazon.com affiliate program is free to do. When you visit the website, you will see a button that says, "Join Now For Free," click on the button, fill out the form with your correct information and you are good to go.

Obviously, you would want to promote products that are related to your blog niche. For instance, if your blog is about entertainment and music, you would want to promote audio equipment, headsets, and other audio items along with visual equipment.

The mistake most bloggers make is that they have a blog in one niche while they promote products in another niche. If you do that, your readers will not take you seriously.

Consider this – if someone is already on your blog reading on a particular topic, and they see an opportunity to purchase something related to that item on Amazon, they would grab the chance. This is one of the reasons Amazon.com affiliate program is great for bloggers.

Most people who read niche blogs are often solution seekers, so if you introduce them to a product that would further provide them with the solution they seek, they would appreciate it. For instance, if you blog about ways of making money online and you promote a book that shows your readers how to set up autoresponders, they would not hesitate to buy the book, thus helping you to earn an affiliate commission.

How to extract your affiliate link

For you to earn money from the sales of a product, you have to extract an affiliate link for that product and use the link when you are making posts on your blog or sending marketing emails. Getting this affiliate link for individual products often seems complicated, especially for beginners. However, it is not really that complicated.

- The first step is to log in to your Amazon affiliate program account.
- Then the second step is to search for the product you want to promote

- Extract their affiliate links.

Let's go over these in details:

Once you have logged into your Amazon affiliate program account, look at the top menu, you will see that next to the "Home" button is a "product linking tab." Hover your mouse over this tab, and there will be a drop-down menu. Select the very first option that says, "product link." Look further down the new page that opens, and you will see a search bar.

Now, enter the keyword for the product you want to promote. For instance, if you wish to promote training boots for men, simply type, "training boots" into the search bar and click "Go."

Once you hit the "Go" button, some search results related to the keywords you typed will be displayed. Next to each search result, you will see an orange button that will provide the affiliate link for that specific product. Click on the arrow next to where it says, "Get link;" when you click on that, you will receive a pop-up box containing the affiliate link to the product.

On close observation, you will notice that the link doesn't really look nice, and if you use the link as it is on your blog, it could be misconstrued as a spam link.

How do you solve this puzzle? On top of the box that pops up, you will see two buttons. One says, "Copy and paste the link below," while the other states, "shorten link with amazon.to." Now, click on the second button, and the affiliate link will be shortened to something more appealing and shorter. There are also other link shortening services that can serve a similar purpose, like bit.ly, etc. Now, include the link thus gotten in your product reviews, YouTube description boxes, social media posts, or any other place where you intend to be generating traffic for your affiliate products. Repeat this process for all the products you want to promote.

How to write a promo post for an affiliate product

When it comes to Amazon affiliate marketing, you must actively promote your affiliate products on your blog for your readers to understand the benefits of the product and hence decide to buy.

For some products, you could consider writing a review post about the product and then include the product's affiliate link in the post. One major problem that people encounter when it comes to writing promo content for affiliate products is that they don't know what to write, especially if they have not used the product in question.

If you want to get ideas on what to write about an affiliate product, your best bet is to visit the Amazon website, search for the product you want to promote, look at five of the top reviews and see what the customers are saying about the product. Usually, customer reviews are honest and will always highlight the benefits, drawbacks of a product. Now, your job is to take all that information and compile it into a very easy to read article and post on your blog.

That's the value you will be providing to your blog visitors. At the end of the article or blog post, include the affiliate link to the product and earn a commission whenever someone buys the product through your link.

Joining the Amazon affiliate program is a great way to earn money with your blog – there are thousands of products that you can promote. What's more? The earning potential is enormous and you get to make some money while you sleep.

Chapter Eleven:

Blog monetization – Digital products (eBooks)

Apart from selling ad space and engaging in affiliate marketing, another way of earning money with your blog is to sell digital products like eBooks and online courses. In fact, eBooks are like hot cakes now – every day, more and more people seek knowledge and if you package information that people seek in the form of an eBook, your readers would be happy to buy.

As a niche blogger, you understand your niche perfectly well – you know those pain points or problems that your readers might have. If you have really been paying attention to your audience, then you would have deduced some of their significant issues. Many times, you may find it hard to compile all the issues into a blog post, so, you might need to compile everything into an eBook.

How do you get eBook topic ideas?

The best way to get eBook topic ideas is to visit Amazon.com, then go to the books/Kindle section. Scroll through the section where you find books related to your niche. Look at the books that are already selling there. Read the reviews left on the books and see what people that have bought the books in the past are saying. Take note of the negative reviews so you can address them in your book.

A platform like Amazon, for instance, allows you to look through the first few pages of a book published on its platform. You can exploit that feature and look at the table of contents of some of the books that have been published in your niche. Use the information you get to form the table of contents for your eBook.

With the table of contents in your hands, you could proceed to start writing your eBook. Make sure that the eBook contains valuable information such that after reading, your readers could say, "wow, I have learned a lot from this."

If you do not have the time to sit and write or if you cannot write lengthy eBooks, you could hire ghostwriters on freelance platforms like Fiverr.com and Upwork.com to help you write an eBook. Usually, you would need to provide the ghostwriter with an outline and discuss other details of the eBook with them.

After writing and publishing your eBook on platforms like Amazon.com and other self-publishing platforms, then it is time to start aggressive marketing of the eBook. You could create a post on your blog to create awareness for the eBook. You could offer the eBook at a discount price for your readers – then ask them to drop a review after reading the book. The reviews will help to improve the ranking of the book and make other people want to read it as well.

Remember, when it comes to making money with eBooks, one book is not enough – you must write as many books as possible. To start seeing reasonable income, you need to have at least five (5) books, and you must market them aggressively to your audience. Since each of the books would be in your niche, you need to link them all up so that customers who buy one could buy the rest of the books.

For each sale of your eBook you record, Amazon takes some part of the money and pay you the rest after a specific period. If you want to avoid this commission that Amazon takes, then you could consider hosting your eBook on your server – then sell it directly on your blog. For this to work, you need to have a payment processor like PayPal or a merchant account.

Once a customer buys the eBook directly from your blog, and you confirm their payment, send them a download link to their eBook. To make the eBook readable on many platforms, convert it into ePub, PDF, Mobi, or any of the other popular eBook formats. You could never go wrong with selling your eBook directly on your platform as you get to keep all the money.

Asides from selling eBook, you could create video courses and sell to your readers. The process is basically the same as that of producing an eBook. You could host the video course directly on your blog and sell to your readers, or you could host it on platforms like udemy.com Lynda.com, etc.

If you do not want to create courses or eBook, you could consider creating a members-only section on your blog. This area will contain gated content or exclusive information that will only be made available to those who pay a subscription fee.

To attract people to join the members-only section, you need to ensure that the general sections on your blog contain valuable information. This way, readers would be longing to see what's in the gated area. It is fundamental human nature – we are always interested or curious to know what's behind the veil. Now, you need to exploit this human nature and make money.

Remember, if people join your members-only section and find out that the information there is something basic they could find elsewhere, they would leave, and that would make your audience displeased. So, you should only create a members-only section if you genuinely have information which you think should not be shared for free.

If you decide to create a members-only section, people could try to guilt-trip you into making everything free. Those are people who think information shouldn't be worth anything. Meanwhile, those same people go to college and pay huge money for the same information. In essence, if you have something of value, don't be shy or guilt-tripped into giving it out for free.

Those who know the value of information will pay anything to have it. If anyone doubts the importance of information and the need for it to be monetized, then that person is not your ideal client anyway, and you should not be worrying yourself with such people. You should be more interested in those who place a premium on valuable information and make sure you provide them with real value.

In this chapter, we have just summarized some passive income methods you could leverage and make money on your blog.

Email marketing to sell more

No matter what you are selling on your blog, you need to grow an email list – your email subscribers are like your loyal customers – you could market any product or service to them, and they would buy. In the online business scene, it is often said that money is in the list and that's true. If you know how to leverage your list, then you can make money selling just anything.

Why is email list so important?

For you to understand why a list is essential, let's analyze how the world of business and sales have evolved over the past years. In the past, a company only needed to develop a good product, then send salespeople to market the products. Those days, customers could buy any product as long as the salesman selling the product is convincing enough.

However, a lot has changed today – the average customer now has a lot of options to choose from. In fact, they are just a Google search away from finding the right products that would solve their problems. In such a world where there are thousands of other people selling the same product that you sell or who offer the same service that you provide, how do you convince the average customer to patronize you and leave your competition? The answer is simple – you need to connect with the customer emotionally.

How do you connect emotionally with the customer? First, you need to understand that today's average customer buys based on emotions and justify logically. So, to make them buy from you, you need to excite them and make them feel emotionally connected to both your product and you as a brand. The only way you could do that is by befriending and communicating with them as friends.

When you constantly communicate with your prospects, readers, or potential customers, the propinquity effect will take its course and make them want to patronize anything you are selling. Apart from creating blog posts, you could communicate with your audience through emails.

With the right lead generation strategy, you could collect the emails of your readers and make sure that you send them the right emails. With the right emails, you could turn your followers or readers into loyal customers who would buy your products and continue to read your blogs.

Having a blog makes email marketing so easy – because you already have an audience – you need to nurture them with emails and warm them up about a product, then market the product to them. Usually, the first stage in email marketing is to acquire a huge audience which could be passed through an autoresponder.

Then the second stage is to use an autoresponder to warm up the vast audience and narrowly segment your list into those who might need your product immediately and those who might need it later. Continue to use a series of email swipes to warm up the subscribers until they are finally ready to buy and then market a product to them. This whole process usually takes time – from the first time that subscribers join your list to the time they are ready to buy. Research shows that it takes up to 7 contacts for a subscriber to be prepared to buy. This means you need to send messages to your potential customers many times before they are finally ready to buy.

Let's get practical

Let's assume that you have created an eBook, and you want to use email marketing to promote and sell this eBook. Here are the steps you need to take:

1. First, you need to use something to attract your potential customers to join your email list. Remember, the fact that someone reads your blog posts does not make the person your customer. At most, the person is just a potential customer, and you need to lure them into joining your email list so you could convert them into customers.

To get your readers to join your email list, you need to use something to lure them. For instance, create a free eBook lead magnet or trip wire and offer it to your readers. It could be a short read that would make them salivate and want more.

The lead magnet or tripwire has to be very captivating so that the reader would be asking for more after reading. The free lead magnet is to prepare the reader to buy the paid eBook or to leave their email in order to receive more information on how to get the paid offer.

2. After creating the lead magnet, make a post on your blog and offer it your readers. You could use other lead generation methods (discussed in the chapter) to provide the lead magnet to your readers.

3. Create a landing page using ClickFunnels or any of the other autoresponders like MailChimp. Once a potential subscriber submits their email to enable them to download the free eBook or offer, send

them a "thank you" message and a link to download their free lead magnet.

4. Now that you have their email; use a series of well-crafted email swipes to inform and educate them about the paid eBook which you want them to buy. Tell them the benefits of the product, and why they need to buy it. Your reasons should be strong enough to make the individual decide to buy. Also, you could include social proofs to further convince prospective customers.

5. Once you have warmed up your leads for some time, introduce them to the product you want to sell to them.

The above approach works like a charm because even if the subscribers do not buy the immediate product you are marketing to them, you still have their email and you could sell other products to them later.

No matter what you are selling on your blog, email marketing will always prove important, and if you learn how to use it well, you will be miles ahead of your competition.

Conclusion

Blogging is dead!!!

I am sure you have heard the above assertion many times – it is usually said by those who jumped into blogging without proper research. Some people have ventured into blogging and were not able to renew their domain name after the first year. Those are the kind of people that make the type of assertion above; as mentioned earlier, they did not do their due diligence before venturing into blogging.

After reading this book, I am sure you have been convinced that blogging is not dead yet and will not die even in the coming years. If there is an online business that will succeed for so long, then it is blogging. Humans are known to be knowledge seekers, and as long as people continue to seek knowledge every day, blogging will continue to be relevant.

However, for you to make it as a blogger, you must be ready to work. Don't be like those who see blogging as a side hustle they could fall back on when they are out of a job. Even though many people have touted blogging as a side job, it is not really a side hustle in the real sense of the word.

Blogging is a full-time affair, and unless you treat it like a full-time business, it will not pay you like a business, and you will likely end up joining those who say it is dead. How many hours do you think it would take to research and come up with a good blogging niche? It could take you up to 5 days or even a week. Would you say that something that takes that amount of time to do is a side hustle?

When you have found a blogging niche, you will need to start designing your blog. If you don't have the resources to hire a web designer, you would need to do the blog customization and development yourself. Again, that will take much of your time. Would you call something that demands such an amount of time a side hustle?

After designing and customizing your blog, you will start doing keyword research for blog posts or articles. After rounds of keywords research, you will need to write insightful posts, and they must be search engine optimized. If they are not keyword optimized, Google and the other search engines will not index them, and your efforts will be in vain.

Writing good and high converting blog posts can take you several hours, if not days – is that what you call a side hustle? So, blogging is not a side hustle; it demands that you give it your full attention. With dedication, hard work, perseverance, you will turn your blog into a money-making machine in no time. Then all the efforts you have been putting into it will start making sense to you.

Blogging is the type of online business that ushers in other online businesses. This means that apart from the regular AdSense program that everyone knows about, you can earn money through affiliate marketing, eBook sales, and many other methods. And when you have established your blog to a certain level, you could dive full time into these other online businesses.

So, as a blogger, your earning potentials are just enormous, and most of the methods of earning are entirely passive. This means you can be making money while you are sleeping. For instance, affiliate marketing is an excellent way of earning money with your blog. And affiliate marketing, if done well, will give you passive income.

EBooks sales is also another way of earning money with your blog, and if done well, following the instructions in this book, can make you a lot of passive income. When you combine all the earning opportunities with a major one like AdSense, you discover that blogging is definitely worth it. You just need to give it time and dedication, and it will turn around to take care of you later.

At first, you will have to work your ass off – you will need to dedicate time to the blog. But as time goes on, the blog will be able to stand on its own. When you have created a reasonable number of posts, which are all ranked on search engines, then you could relax and start reaping the results of your efforts.

Also, when you have grown the blog to a certain level, you could start outsourcing some of your operations to freelancers. For instance, you could outsource keyword research and writing of articles to freelancers so that you can have time for other essential aspects of your business or life. You can find good freelancers on fiverr.com and upwork.com.

Printed in Great Britain
by Amazon